JUDY: A SECOND CHANCE

SHE

REFUSED TO

GIVE UP

The story of Judy Mbugua
Her struggle with the dilemmas of early
marriage, her education cut short,
and how she resolved to change
the course of her life

by
Judy Mbugua
with Connie Kisuke

Judy: A Second Chance

Published by

PRECISE Communications Limited

Valley Road

P.O. Box 59004, Nairobi, Kenya

Scripture quotations are from

New International Version NIV

copyright © 1973, 1978, 1984

by International Bible Society,

and Living Bible.

Cover Design by Word Alive

Layout Artist, Peter Mulwale

Printed by Kijabe Press, P.O. Box 40 Kijabe.

JUDY: A SECOND CHANCE

CONTENTS

FOREWORD

by
Luis Bush
International Director, AD 2000 Movement

In "Second Chance", you will be caught up in the amazing story behind this woman of God. As Judy spoke forth at the press conference we shared some time back in South Africa, I thought to myself, *here is a Christian woman who speaks with authority.* This power comes not only from words and life's journey, but also from a present position of serious authority, made manifest in three ways:

First, Judy's authority comes from accepting who she is in Christ who is in her. Second, she lives her life with authority because of her love for people. She has experienced a full-orbed dosage of pain from her journey through life. As you get caught up in her journey while reading this book, you will realize that the struggles of life cab be used to gain eternal understanding, strengthen vision and resolve that seeks to add to, not detract from the purpose of earthly journey. Third, you sense the authority in her via the boldness with which she speaks forth issues related to justice. On one occasion, I heard Judy speak of the horrors of the practice of female circumcision in Africa today. On another occasion, vastly outnumbered in the room by Christian men from around the world, she pointedly addressed the need and importance of giving the women their proper place in Christian ministry. Whatever the issue, Judy will articulate her position with clarity, passion and authority.

Judy's spiritual insights astound great Christian leaders of our day. Her gripping story, so beautifully, yet frankly presented in "Second Chance", ignites hope in the heart of any woman, man or young person. It prompts Christians never to give up, regardless of past failures or future pressures. Never give up never, never, never. That is the powerful message of "Second Chance". By the end of the book, you will encounter why Judy became enamoured with God - the One who is able to do immeasurably more than all that you could ask or imagine, according to the power that lives within you. As the chairperson of the AD2000 Women's Track, her life and ministry has modeled what God can do through a woman who is totally yielded to christ. Thank you judy, for giving us a glimpse of the greatness of our God gained through the submission of our life to Him.

FOREWORD

by
Rev. Dennis White
Senior Pastor, Nairobi Pentecostal Church

The Judy Mbugua's story is a commentary of God's Grace. To those who know the author, what is particularly thrilling is to see the continuing miracle of God's Grace at work in her.

After many years of Christian ministry, I am convinced that the ministry of encouragement is needed more than ever among Christians today. I am also convinced that God's plan for providing us with these vital and valuable instruments of encouragement is by the tailor-made process.

Judy's cultural background, her early mistakes and hard-knocks, her search for reality, her quest for knowledge, her slow to surface talents and abilities and her intense yearning for God provided the Divine Designer with the ample materials for a master piece in encouragement.

So may the purpose of this volume be realized. May Judy's pilgrimage from bare-foot school girl in Kikuyu land, Kenya, to God's ambassador in pulpits around the world, lead us to the realization that the wonders of God's Grace are awesome and available to all who trust Him.

INTRODUCTION

by
Rev. Dr. Tokunboh Adeyemo
General Secretary, Association of
Evangelicals in Africa

A SECOND CHANCE is a FAT story. It is an incredible story of a humble lady who is Faithful, Available and Teachable. With such trademarks, there is no limit to how far one can be used by God to accomplish His Kingdom purpose.

For over fifteen years now, I have been privileged to have a close acquaintance with Judy, her husband and family, being members of the same local church. For eight of those years, we have been serving together as staff of the Association of Evangelicals in Africa (AEA). As a team we have had the pleasure to run workshops, organize seminars, conduct missions, direct meetings and address conferences together throughout Africa as well as beyond Africa.

Countless are the times we wept together in prayers with deep agony and rejoiced together as we witnessed God deliver His miracles. We still do. In all of my interactions with Judy, I have found her to be reliable, ambitious and trustworthy. Very early in our acquaintance,

I enlisted her as one of my very few prayer partners. When Judy says "I will remember you in my prayers," you can trust her.

When the Lord led her to the AEA in 1989 as a full-time continental coordinator of our Movement's Women Commission called PACWA, she made a big sacrifice in terms of material benefits, privilege and positional power. Knowing that her call was from the Lord, she never grumbled. For the eight years she has faithfully and diligently served the Lord, the church throughout the world and humanity in general. Her addition to our team at the AEA has brought us nothing but growth, expansion, spiritual depth, recognition, especially in many government circles, and sharpened vision.

Making her story available in a book form, I know, is to serve one purpose: To bring glory to God as every reader is encouraged to believe God saying, "if God did for Judy, He will do it for me too".

Judy Mbugua

PREFACE

Several people who have heard my testimony have asked me to write a book on the story of my life. My children and sisters also have asked me to do so, but I have always been reluctant. At one point my sister Vicky said she would have to write it. My daughter insisted if I didn't write it she would. This persuaded me to write this book. So I started writing it in 1986. But then I began to feel like I was opening wounds that were beginning to heal, so I put it aside after a few chapters.

Early in 1993, I was having a chat with Mrs. Connie Kisuke, the then Managing Editor of *Step Africa Magazine*. During the course of our conversation I shared a bit about my past and some of my experiences. Then she said to me, "Judy, why don't you write your story?" Connie had earlier served as the PACWA chairperson of communications committee in the 1989 Conference, and now, as *Step* operated under AEA, we were serving under the same organisation.

Later she shared with me that she felt called to write some books, but for my story, she still would encourage me to write it. Then on a light note, I asked her "Why don't you do it? I would appreciate you writing my book." After some time she was convinced she could do it. We therefore agreed that I "tell the story", in a draft form, then she would look at it and work from there. It has taken more than just a draft and working from there. It has taken a lot of discussions, interviews, hard thinking, weighing in advance the different sides of the impact some information might have on the reader and the market, listening to the views of others, piecing together information from cuttings and so forth.

Now the book has come to be and we are glad we talked and the Lord gave us unity of mind and spirit. We have prayed in agreement as several attacks from the enemy have confronted either one or both of us during the various stages of its development. The Lord has, nevertheless, seen the work through, and we are grateful to Him.

In the process of sharing the story of my life, my aim has been inevitable to touch other people's lives and to encourage them, especially the family. I hope and pray that none of what I share will hurt anybody, though that is hard to safeguard. I am quite sensitive to hurting and because of this, I have had to leave out some chunks of the story.

It is not my intention to prominently portray self, but it is also hard to show or tell how God dealt with someone without the person being portrayed in the centre of the events, for He is revealed in how He deals with us. And how can I extract myself from the picture, and still show how the Lord worked in miraculous ways, to give me a second chance - hence the regular mention of me in this process, but ultimately in order to glorify Christ in me, who has become my all in all.

Finally after much struggle in writing the book, I did not understand why I did not feel pushed to go to the press. So I decided to pray more and wait. The questions uppermost in my mind being why do I feel that this book will be a big blessing to those about to give up, yet by writing it I would be exposing my personal life?

Now I know why the delay. The lord had a better plan and perfect timing for this book. He was waiting to save my husband so that we can both rejoice in His accomplished work.

After 28 years of prayer for my husband's salvation, one day, without much fanfare he knelt down in our bedroom and accepted the Lord. Just like that. It was not the way I expected. I had always planned it in my mind that he would get saved the Pentecostal style, and in Nairobi Pentecostal church where we have been for the last 25 years. I thought it would be time for me and friends to shout hallelujah. But no, quietly in his own gentle way he accepted Jesus, at home with just the two of us.

I started calling the children to tell them about it, then he said "Judy, this is my testimony and not yours!" Soon after I was invited to speak in Holland in the family week of Broadcasting Corp. My topic was to be 'Living with unsaved spouses', I asked him, "what will I tell them now that you are saved?"

He said "Tell them the truth".

Judy Mbugua

Acknowledgement

I would like to acknowledge with great appreciation the several people who have made such indelible marks on my life, and to whom I am greatly indebted. There are many that I cannot mention due to the limitation of this book. But to all of you, who have been praying for me, I say, thanks. However, let me mention the following:

My husband, Richard, has taught me to love. In this ministry he has encouraged me to live to my full potential. Dick, may you be richly blessed. Thank you for giving me to God to serve Him. I know there is a share of the heavenly reward for you for your contribution in this ministry.

My children - I could never exchange any of you for anything in the world.

Dr. Tokunboh Adeyemo - you have been used of God to encourage, challenge and train me. Thank you for believing in me when most doubted, and thank you for encouraging me in the ministry. Your testimony helped me to make the decision to leave my permanent and pensionable job in order to serve on full-time basis. Your kind of faith is contagious!

All my Pastors, particularly Pastor Dennis White. You are one among few who truly know how to make the difference in confusing situations. You have believed in

Acknowledgement

me too, encouraged me and given me opportunities to serve in the body of Christ.

All my faithful prayer partners, in particular Eunice Gathithi. The whole LHSF committee - each of you mean so much to me and you have been a great blessing. PACWA Executive Committee, especially Eva, Esme and Sophie. Mrs. Everlyn Christensen, who took me in as a spiritual daughter - thank you Mom. Mrs. Lorry Lutz - my prayerful prayer partner. If I continue, I will fill many pages, so let me thank each one of you at the Nairobi Pentecostal Church who mean so much to me. Also my very special precious bosses Prof. Peter Gacii and Ian Rayner, who believed in me so much they provided ladders for me to climb up though training and in the Lords' work.

Finally my appreciation go to my co-writer and editor of this book. Thank you Connie for taking up this writing project. For the interest and dedication you have shown, and for spending countless hours on it. May the Lord reward you.

Then to you Margaret Anaminyi and Rosemary Gitonga, for your very keen eyes in spotting and correcting the so commonly overlooked errors and your helpful suggestions that have added to the shape of this book, thank you and the Lord bless you richly.

From those of us who have seen and listened to her

Leadership becomes her! Even as she ran around barefoot growing up in the rural Kenyan village, she influenced others with her strong will and infectious sense of humour. Headstrong and rebellious, she defied her family's cultural standards and Christian teaching. She fell in love with Richard at an early age. But God saw the potential in this capable young African woman — He gave her a second chance to make her a powerful tool for the gospel across the continent and the world.

Judy has been beautifully open and vulnerable in sharing her heart. The reader will understand something of the richness and complexity of the African culture by reading Judy's life story, and will appreciate Judy's experiences and growth in the light of her background. This book will convince every reader that God is willing to give a "Second Chance" to anyone who comes to Him in repentance and obedience.

Lorry Lutz
International Coordinator; AD 2000 Women's Track
****

What a privilege and blessing it has been to know Judy Mbugua. She has been a voice for African women from whom we seldom hear.

I heard her at the great WEF Assembly in Canada and a few weeks later she was with us at Global Commission On World Evangelization (GCOWE) at Pretoria, South Africa, as one of the leaders of the AD 2000 & Beyond Movement.

This unusual book about what God has done in her life, and I am hoping that thousands of men and women around the world will not only read it, but also get involved in distributing it to others.

In world missions, women are at the cutting edge, but often in other situations women are not being released for ministry as they should. I hope this book will help release many more. We men need to do our part.

George Verwer
International Director Operation Mobilisation
****

A SECOND CHANCE is a FAT story. It is an incredible story of a humble lady who is Faithful, Available, and Teachable. With such trademarks, there is no limit to how far one can be used by God to accomplish His Kingdom purpose.

Rev. Dr. Tokunboh Adeyemo
General Secretary; Association of Evangelicals in Africa
****

Judy Wanjiru Mbugua (or simply), Judy is one person whose pursuit and zeal for God has left imprints in the lives of many, especially in Kenya. This has been particularly evident across the great generation and spiritual divide between the young and the old where Judy (most likely unaware) has played the spiritual "arbitrator" role with remarkable success.

In order to appreciate the significance of Judy's "arbitrator" role, it is necessary to understand the dilemma facing the youth in the late 1960s through the 80s in Kenya. The youth was caught up in a difficult triangular balancing act involving traditional beliefs, conventional religion and an ambition for personal socioeconomic advancement. Very few of the older generation seemed to understand or appreciate the struggle encountered by the youth. The youth needed a contemporary and exemplary Christian mentor to relate to, to emulate - a Christian whose zeal and witness for Christ was evident across the great generation and spiritual divide.

Mrs. Judy Mbugua became such a mentor for many young Christians like myself during this difficult period. She was, and still is a true demonstration of uncompromising faith in, and love for the Lord Jesus coupled with natural exuberant joy and unique regenerate personality that transcended the generation gap.

Sammy Murimi
One of the young of the times whom she has touched

The Judy Mbugua's story is a commentary of God's Grace. To those who know the author, what is particularly thrilling is to see the continuing miracle of God's Grace at work in her.

Pastor Dennis White
Senior Pastor; Nairobi Pentecostal Church

DEDICATION

This book is lovingly dedicated to my late Dad, Mzee Hosea Wainaina, who encouraged and challenged me to work hard and be somebody. It is also dedicated to the countless would be successful young girls and women who may be wallowing in self-pity after seeming failures. My message to all of you is, wake up! Failure is not final. Our God is a God of Second, Third and Countless chances. Never give up.

CHAPTER ONE

STATE GUEST

The plane touched the grounds of Blantyre Airport, Malawi, our host country and home for the next one week. My attention was drawn to the voice of our flight Chief Steward through a Public Address.

"Attention please, Ladies and Gentlemen, hold onto your seats for a while. We have on our flight some V.I.P. passengers, kindly let us give them a few minutes to alight first."

The four ladies I was with and I held onto our seats. Silence followed. Our curious eyes turned from side to side searchingly. The minutes ticked by. No one moved, no one stood. After some time our curiosity turned to impatience. Where are the V.I.Ps? Who could they be? I wondered silently. Then, I noticed the steward walking down the isle, looking at me with a smile. He made a bow beckoningly. I was dumbfounded.

"Madam," he spoke, "can you please lead your delegation out of the plane?"

A little confused, I hesitated. Perhaps the V.I.Ps had gone out through a different exit and we were now delaying the routine landing procedures of the crew. But this wasn't it, I was to discover sooner, to my utter surprise, that the

V.I.Ps were none other than the four of us; the Nairobi based members of the Continental Council of the Pan African Christian Alliance (PACWA). The steward must have noticed my bewilderment, for he explained that we were State Guests and he had instructions that he should let us out of the plane first. While all the other passengers watched to see who the V.I.P. guests were, I led my delegation of women out of the plane.

"Oh, I am not used to this kind of treatment!", exclaimed one of the ladies.

"Don't worry," I told her, "just follow me and walk with dignity!"

I said the words to instill confidence among my fellow ladies and to give myself the right pose and attitude for the present encounter. We descended the steps to an awaiting reception of beautiful bouquets of flowers. We were escorted to the V.I.P lounge, not even being allowed to carry our own hand luggage! We were entertained with more refreshments.   "What a treat, what a luxury," I wondered silently.

I made myself comfortable and anticipated the next surprise, whatever it would be. This treatment must be a prelude to many more, I concluded in my thoughts. Soon, the delegation was led to meet the Head of State, His Excellency, the then Malawi's life President, Ngwazi Dr. H. Kamuzu Banda, who was to officially launch the Pan African Christian Women Alliance. This was to be the first regional conference, held from 24th to 31st August 1991, at the Great Hall, at Chancellor College in Zomba, Malawi's academic capital.

We were taken to Zomba on arrival. On the third day we were seated as State guests in the main State House with the beaming and clicking of cameras of the press crew focused on us. I was drawn into the limelight and suddenly, without prior warning, I was put on the spot, and for a short while, as it were, made the "Honorable Minister" for "Women and Family Affairs in Africa."

I found myself at the centre of high profile discussions with His Excellency and our conversation was being broadcast live. I had no prior preparation for this session, nor did I anticipate it. So, of course, I had no written speech or point notes to refer to. But there I was, responding to pertinent issues affecting women and families in Africa. The following day newspapers had quotes of what I had said. This created a mirage of curiosity among the people of the press as well as the general public. So many of them wanted to meet me and know more about me.

This encounter reminded me of another experience I had, not too long before this. Just before the Malawi conference, I had been to Nigeria to launch a pre-PACWA programme. Whenever my hosts introduced me, they kept giving me high-flying titles. Either due to their assumption that Nationally organized meetings are led by top personalities, or what they believed I should be, I was often referred to as either Dr. Judy Mbugua or Rev. Mbugua. At the close of each meeting, I had to make a humble submission that I had no doctoral qualifications nor was I an ordained Minister. Nevertheless, I have come to accept that, God had seen it fit to place me among the rank and file of those who have earned those titles in order to fulfill his chosen purpose for me. I must admit though, that this has happened without any ambitious efforts or strategic manoeuvre on my part. How did I come to this level of service?

In this book I am going to share my story with the hope that God will use it to help, challenge and strengthen someone who may be discouraged and lost in the midst of difficult circumstances. Times do come in life, as I have discovered, when one wonders whether God can really come in into an individual's hopeless situation and speak something that turns that individual's situation all round to a meaningful, fulfilling and sometimes a real adventure with Him.

Every story has a beginning. My story too, has a beginning, a beginning which is truly a mixture of pain and sorrow, joy and sadness, weakness and trength, poverty and plenty, struggle and success.

My background may seem ordinary to some. It may, I guess, seem promising to others. Still to others, it may emit some sparks of peculiarity. Whichever way it may seem, I believe it is through this background that the Lord shaped me to fit into His framework of what He would take me through. Some of the experiences I have had to go through may be considered mistakes or tragedy. But nevertheless, the Master used them as a furnace, to purify me, then in His power transformed them into His glorious purposes. He is the Master Potter, the Sovereign Lord, and He does what He wills with the clay.

CHAPTER TWO

FATHER'S "ABDUCTION" TURNS TO EDUCATION OPPORTUNITY

Missing Records, a puzzle to solve.

How can you not know my exact birth date and yet I am your first born daughter?" I faced my mother with the daring question. My mind was full of frustration and my heart full of determination. I wanted to know the answer. It was one afternoon around 1988. We were seated refreshing our minds about the first wedding I ever attended. It was not only my first wedding but I was honoured to be one of the flower girls of the wedding, yet I had no shoes. So this was another issue that I confronted my mother with, why couldn't my parents buy me shoes even for an important occasion like that one and yet they were rich?

My mind flashed back to that memorable day in 1954. Just a day before the wedding my dad and I had driven from house to house in the village looking for shoes for a little girl. I remember it was like a mini drama.

"*Hodi!* "(May we come in) dad would cautiously announce our presence while we stood outside, and indicate our wish to be allowed into a house.

"Do you have shoes that can fit a little girl?" He would ask and then push me forward so that the people could see me as we entered the house.

House after house and the answer was "no, sorry." In the end we got a pair of boys shoes which was several sizes bigger than my feet. At that point there was no choice whether I should wear boys' shoes or not. The question of the size was no big deal. Somehow they had to be made to fit. By the ingenuity of the village folk, papers were stuffed in the shoes to fill the spaces where my feet could not reach until they accommodated my size of feet. I was then given a walking rehearsal in them until I gained confidence. Come the day of the wedding! It was an ordeal I lived to remember. The make believe style of shoes didn't seem to work right. I was literally pulling the shoes and trudging along throughout the procession. But the day was done nevertheless, and I gained the experience of being a flower girl.

As I recalled the incident, it bothered me that my parents

who owned a car then had not bought me a pair of shoes. My mother was at pains to explain. But as for me, whatever the reason, I needed to know. Finally she explained that during that period (1952-1963), the colonial government had declared a State of Emergency due to political reasons. Together with it was a rule that for any one to travel to town, he or she had to secure a permit. Permits were only given for valid reasons. However, since validity was sanctioned by the same authority that dictated the terms or reasons to secure a permit, whichever way one approached it, both permit and validity were governed the colonial interests. It therefore followed, unfortunately for me, that going to town to buy a pair of shoes for a little African girl was not a valid reason for a permit.

That question settled, I was yet to get an answer to the question of my birth date. My parents were among the few well to do in the village by the time I was born. In addition to that, my father was one of the few highest educated in that village. I knew I was not only a daughter of a renown teacher, but I was, unlike many of my peers, born in a hospital, a privilege only a few babies had at that time.

It was the presence of my brother in this second part of the "confrontation" of that moment that saved the day. He said the date of my birth was 9th November. That somehow helped a little, I had the date and month, if not the year, at least somewhere to begin. I began to observe 9th November as my birthday until some years later when I decided once and for all to sort out the jigsaw puzzle.

I had been told of the mission hospital where I was born. I therefore decided to do a search. I visited Kikuyu Mission

Hospital one day. After explaining my mission to the hospital administrator, I found favour with her. I was given a whole file with registration of births. I searched through vehemently, but to my dismay I couldn't find my mother's name in that file. For a moment I stood puzzled, doubtful whether the administrator gave me the right file. But by all indications it was the right file. So I thought hard and suddenly something struck me.

My father, it occurred to me, was commonly known by his Christian name, Hosea. I quickly went to the file and shuffled through, checked under letter 'H', then wow! There it was, in black and white, Mrs. Hosea, and her baby girl, dated 3rd November 1947. Thanks to good record keeping, the baby file of 1947 referred to again in 1989 marked the end of my most critical childhood questions. Why did I struggle so much just for the whys and hows of trivial matters like having no shoes or not knowing my birth date? This year in particular, I had already known what God wanted to do with me. I needed first of all to understand a bit of who I was. I had also felt that my story might be important in the future, as I felt God wanted to use it too. So I did not want to go on with some gaps in my life that seemed important, yet unfilled, and only my parents were in a position to fill them, now there was only one living parent, and she was old. Wisdom would dictate I take advantage while she still had breath.

Apart from my parents not keeping records carefully, I believe I was born to some of the best parents in the world. They were very loving and raised us up in the best way possible. At the time of my birth and growing up, circumstances and attitudes towards bringing up and educating girls were not quite positive. Cultural norms received and unchallenged from generations past categorized girls as assets whose value was determined by the number of cows that would be fetched as dowry, as well as how many children she bore in her lifetime as a wife. My parents' attitudes and views were different and only shared by a very small minority in our country then. How my parents managed against all odds to keep and practice different norms I cannot tell, but I experienced total acceptance and was as valued as my brothers were. We were nine children, four boys and five girls. And as far as I know, my parents gave us equal rights and considerations in every way. For this, I will ever appreciate them and thank God for them.

Education

My father was a product of a mixed marriage between a Kikuyu father and a Maasai mother. His parents' marriage was one of the occasional incidentals during those days, which used to happen during the tribal conflicts between the two tribes. The Maasai legendary heritage gave them the "rights" to all cattle under the sun. And to them rustling to capture the supposedly stray cattle was in order. This was the main reason for tribal confrontations. The invaders would of course be resisted. During such confrontation the conquering tribe would not only capture the cattle but would capture young beautiful girls and women, who would be carried over and become wives to the different men as the tribal elders would decide. Rarely did such women try to find their way back home. This was often one of the situations women accepted as a reality of the day without question. That is how my grandfather got his wife.

My dad's father didn't live long. He died when his son

was still very young. The British had began to introduce formal education to the African children in early 1900s. As had now been perceived by the Africans, this was an imposition of the white man's culture onto the Africans. Worse, education was being viewed with suspicion. Most parents saw it as a trick devised to turn the African children against their parents and their culture. Why, for instance, should African children be taken away from their important responsibilities of looking after cattle and working in the fields to go and learn the white man's way of life and propaganda? Every well meaning father resisted the idea of education to Africans. Thus, it was how they "protected" their own children from going to the white man's school.

The "unfortunate children", however, were those without fathers to protect them. The white man literally abducted them to school. My father fell into this category, and this is how he "accidentally" went to school. The white man already had a specific category of schools as well as the curriculum designed for Africans. The final goal, as it turned out, was to fit a few Africans into the colonial administrative and social system to assist as clerks, teachers, hospital assistants and so forth. All things worked for good for my father, who proved very brilliant and took advantage of the opportunity. He did very well and proceeded to Alliance High School, one of the best schools in our country to this day. He was one among a few in his area who was now highly educated. The level he reached was by that time the highest attainable for an African man of the time within our area. After the formal education he qualified to join a teacher training college and became a teacher, again one of the enviable careers of the time. He performed so well as a teacher that he was promoted to Inspector of schools in his home district of Limuru. This turned out for our advantage as his children.

My father had learnt the value of education, so he saw to it that all his children had a chance to go to School. In my family there was no gender discrimination, so the sons as well as daughters had equal opportunity.

In January 1954, I formally started school. Like all children starting school, I had the first love excitement, but it was short-lived. Although I had what it feels to be in school earlier, for my father used to take me to school with him occasionally, and the school environment had therefore become familiar to me, it was good only while it lasted, since I only paid occasional visits to school where my main occupation was playing and enjoying the interaction with other pupils as they went through the classroom procedure. Come the day I was finally enrolled and I had to begin going to school daily in the chilly cold mornings, it became a nightmare. I began to realize how warm my bed was in the morning.

The very thought of waking early every day used to send cold shivers down my spine. Within a short time I was no longer interested. School life was now totally a new way of life which required high discipline. The struggle to keep this discipline was not always successful and I began to have trouble with my teachers because I often got to school late.

There were three other enemies in my new way of life: The morning dew, the hard prickly grass and small sharp stones on the path I trod. The latter were commonplace in this path which worsened the situation due to the condition of my feet. My village was rife with jiggers, that often, attacked little feet mercilessly and I wasn't spared. Apart from the ordeal of the pain experienced through the method used by our aunties and moms to remove the jiggers, painful itchy openings on the skin were the result.

On my way to school, I used to have the nasty experience where the wet dew would enter the post-jigger openings making the feet so much more painful. I would also be pricked by the hard grass and hit by sharp small stones. Even though this experience was unwelcome, I knew at the back of my mind that school was, nevertheless, good and important. There were aspects of it that I loved and enjoyed, such as learning to read and write, playing and the sing- sing times. Further, it had been hammered to all of us by my father that education was very vital in our lives and for our future success. Soon I learnt to appreciate it all and settled down to learn and succeed.

I Dared the Boys' Domain

I progressed well in school with little struggles. I was enjoying learning new things as well as the school's atmosphere of learning especially the philosophy of competition in performance. In my school, academic excellence was emphasized and was reinforced by teachers through the regulated competitions among the pupils in each class. It was a mixed school, and in those days it was theoretically believed that only boys could achieve the highest marks in the competition. The attitude was reinforced indirectly by the larger majority of the school population, some teachers included. Some subjects, for instance Mathematics, General Science, Geography, Civics and so forth, were seen as exclusively boys' stuff. Girls were expected to concentrate on Domestic Science, Cooking and Knitting. Many girls then shrunk at the idea of competition with boys on those subjects that were "for boys only".

I defied this trend of exclusive subjects right away. I did not even care for the existing attitudes on that. My father had always told me I could do as well as anybody else. I determined to compete with boys on those "special subjects", indeed I competed in all of the subjects offered and nullifying the false theories regarding girls' imposed inabilities and boys' abilities, I excelled. My parents were very proud of me. I also took interest in physical activities and was involved in Net Ball, Cycling, Long Jump and High jump. Today I still have my awards won during the school and inter-school sports competitions.

I completed my primary and intermediate school in 1961 and passed the Kenya Preliminary Examination with Credits in English and Mathematics. With that, I felt quite accomplished. It was however, my father's wish for me to proceed with further education, but this was not my priority. I wanted to spread my wings further. A job was more appealing to me at the time and opted for a job. I got one as an untrained teacher immediately, and not long after, I set my eyes on the man of my dreams. I could never have guessed that, not too far into the future, I would be crying bitter tears, regretting the decision I made. I never imagined that I would later spend sleepless nights and long days, while nursing children at the same time struggling with books, and pay dearly to get the further education I so easily dismissed as unimportant, in preference for a job.

CHAPTER THREE

COME WE STAY

"She was only sixteen,
only sixteen, and I loved her so,
She was too young to fall in love,
And I was too young to know."

This was one of the hit love songs in the sixties and one of my favourite. I used to sing it a lot. Hardly did I think it would happen to me. This was in 1963. I was exactly sixteen when I met a man and both of us fell head over heels in love. I had never met him before. I wonder whether I would have met him at all had he not been sent on relief duties at the railway station near the school where I taught.

He was a Station Master working with the East African Railways. On this memorable day, I had taken the pupils out for Nature Study as was set out in the lesson plan of that day. In such a lesson, one would be expected to take the class to the open field where they would see natural vegetation and animals they were taught about. This made their practicals and experiential learning. Instead of going to the open field, I decided to take my class to the Railway

Station for a change, to learn something about the trains and the railway system.

In those days, a visit of pupils with their teacher to a Government establishment for learning purposes was a welcome gesture, at times one needed not make an appointment in advance. Although I expected there would be someone manning the station to show us around and explain to the class the different aspects of the station and the locomotives, I did not anticipate that the person who happened to be on duty then would steal my heart so suddenly, and grip it so powerfully.

As soon as I looked at Richard, and he looked at me, our eyes were glued to each other. He was charming and handsome. When it came to asking questions, I suppose I asked more questions about him than the children asked him about locomotives. Before the visit was concluded, a dinner date was set. Ours was love at first sight.

Before many days were over since that first meeting, we were so engrossed with each other we could think of nothing in the world as beautiful as being together. Soon I got into the family way. At that time this didn't bother any of us, it seemed quite normal. Richard and I knew almost instinctually that we wanted to get married to each other and, we determined to get married, come rain or sunshine.

We thought marriage was as easy as falling in love. We were wrong, for when my parents learnt about my pregnancy and desire to get married they were mad. To them I was too young to even fall in love, let alone be a mother or think of getting married. This parental disposition was completely opposed to my thinking and desire. As far as I was concerned, I was ready for marriage, and the man I wanted to marry wanted to marry me as much as I wanted to marry him. I had to learn later that not only was my age the greatest problem, but the area where my suitor came from was also an issue to reckon with; it was near the city and people who were born and brought up near the big city were considered "spoilt". Then ensued a struggle I had never anticipated, which I thought would choke my very being to nothingness.

For two years my dad detained me at home. At a later stage he even decided to move his whole family to Nakuru where he had bought a farm. He forced me to stay in the farm in order to reduce my proximity to Richard, or perhaps hoping my interests would wane. But that made matters even worse, as any teenager in the circumstances, I became more curious and more calculative. Somehow the two of us found our own secret ways of meeting.

Richard's parents visited our home after I had my second child, intending to fulfill the customary obligations to show that they were interested in my being their son's wife, and they gave something for the initial dowry. In spite of this, matters continued to drag.

I became more and more impatient. I wondered what gain there would be to continue living in my parents' home and rearing children without the father. Not that their father had declined to take up the parental responsibility, he was ready for them and for me. And on my part, I was already torn apart wanting to be with him as his wife, for that is what we were convinced I was, not just his girlfriend. After much thought I took the daring decision once and for all, with or without my parents consent, to get married. I ran away and joined Richard in 1965.

At long last I was with my sweetheart, my husband now. That day the stars shone brightly and the moon smiled at us with joy, the sun too greeted our day happily, that's what we felt. We were so very happy together at last, and for good, nothing mattered now. Little did I think of the stormy reaction that would follow from my parents; they were extremely hurt.

At the back of my mind I knew my parents would have loved to send me off with a church wedding and the accompanying blessings. But their reaction to the action I took was clear. I had not only defied my early Christian teaching but I had ran away to marry a man from the "wrong place," Kabete. The latter did not worry me much, but considering my Christian up- bringing, I felt guilty. I later wrote them a letter to apologize for having ran away without their consent. They gladly forgave me. It was such a relief. Four years later my husband and I formalized our marriage in church.

Reality

There is one thing I know for sure, and that is my love for Richard is as real and genuine today, as it was the first day I met him. I am also sure too, of his love for me since then to this day. The only difference between then and now is that then, my youthful passion and fantasies led me to think life would thrive on love alone. I soon discovered, to my shock, it wasn't so. Even when two people who are madly in love are finally together and have overcome all parental "prisons", life demands more than love. One needs food, clothes, shelter and other basic necessities, and this means struggle, sometimes painful struggle. There are also social and spiritual needs to be met for life to be complete.

In my youthful ignorance I thought love was enough to cover all. I believe this attitude was shaped and influenced more by romantic novels, which I read so much, especially Denise Robins. The stories always ended with, "and they lived happily ever after".

When I got married, I had to quit my teaching job to join my husband at Murang'a where he worked. We had already two children to care for by the time I moved and there was only one small salary from my husband's side to cater for all our family needs and the two children's needs. Shortly after, other children followed, each year without giving us a break. Taking care of two or three children who followed one another so closely would depress anybody, just figure out that kind of responsibility for a young mother, with not only two or three children. But even then, for me, it was not just the mother's care that was the issue, but the adjustment was too difficult to cope with. While at my parents' home there was always someone to take care of me and to help. Here I was, now not only required to take care of the children, but also be a wife and manager of a home.

There was another thing too difficult to bear the shortages. We could barely meet the cost of our basic daily needs. At my parent's home I never knew what it was to lack food, clothing or school fees. Here there was an income hardly enough for one person, yet I was supposed to stretch it to cover all the needs in this family, I could not. Although my husband entrusted me with all his salary, leaving himself with only a small amount for his pocket money, the end result was that before the middle of each month, the money would run out. I would be frustrated and somehow he would struggle to ensure we at least had food to sustain us to the next pay day. Soon, however, this began to strain our relationship. He thought I was careless and I felt he was uncaring.

There was still another strain - washing his clothes. I had never washed a man's trousers in my life. Life was made harder for me in this area because the firm where he worked provided them with Khaki uniforms, white in colour. It was expected that these be kept very clean and ironed very well. Being the good wife I wanted and was expected to be, I tried cleaning my husband's uniform with some good success. But when it came to ironing his uniform, I did a thoroughly bad job. One had to press them in such a way that clear stiff folds would show on the top centre of the sleeves in the case of shirts and on the front centre of the knees in the case of trousers. The day I began, I pressed the wrong way and clear nice folds showed on the sides. When my husband came home he was horrified. Then he thought it humorous and started laughing. I felt so stupid that I cried. Then he kindly began to teach me how to iron trousers. He went further and taught me a few more things including washing shirts and cooking ugali.

Dilemma

Life went on like this for about two years, then I began to be disillusioned with life, I began to have some serious questions. Is that all there was to life? What had become of my dreams and imaginations about life and marriage?

Here I was, a young mother with no skill or training of any sort which would enable me at least engage in a trade or job to help improve on our income, and here we were, a very needy family with only one person to support financially, but limited by the amount of income, yet with an able bodied partner, who was hampered by lack of skill and a job. There seemed to be no future prospects in view. My questions were unending; where was I going from here? How were we going to raise all our children on one small salary from my husband's employment?

I began to reminisce my youth. Often I would spend days crying and wishing I had listened to my parents and waited until I had a good education and training of some sort. I thought of my friends who had continued with education. I assessed their future prospects and knew we were incomparable. This was about the time they were getting married and their future seemed prospective if not better. They had acquired good education and some training which gave them a better footing in life. As for me, I was already married and almost over with getting children - I already had four and expecting the fifth, not sure whether their food, clothing and schooling would be guaranteed. This was horrifying at best. What was I to do next? I constantly questioned and torrents of tears would wash my face, anguish would threaten to tear my heart into pieces.

After some time I knew I couldn't go on like that. Something had to be done. My husband and I had to face the challenge realistically. We discussed the matter and reached a conclusion that it would be best for me and the children to go to Kabete, his parents' up-country home. There were two major reasons for this: I had decided to

41

get some training on secretarial skills and Kabete was near Nairobi City where I could be attending college. His parents owned a piece of land there and he was entitled to his share where he could construct a house of his own. He had not constructed one yet.

We then decided to put up a house quickly before the move to Kabete. This was a very expensive undertaking but given our circumstances it was the only way out. We did not take any chances for delays so we moved forward in action. My husband had to withdraw all his savings to carry on with the construction work. Within a short time our three- roomed timber house stood, ready to be occupied. A pit latrine and bathroom were constructed outside our house.

CHAPTER FOUR

KABETE - HERE WE COME

It was one cold July day in 1966 when Richard put us, the children and I, on a bus from Murang'a to Kabete, to begin our new life. I was determined to make our life different. Yet as I anticipated having to settle in Kabete, a cold wave of apprehension and nostalgia filled my heart. My mind flashed back to my first visit to my husband's parents in 1965. The incident had left me with unpleasant memories.

I was en-route from my parents' home in Nakuru where I had gone to visit my father who was very sick and nearing his death. I had written him a letter before to ask him for his forgiveness for marrying without his consent, which he had graciously granted. Yet I felt obliged to go personally and talk over the matter and ensure all was well between us before his death. I went along with my youngest and second born child. I was, however, expecting my third child any time during this trip. But I reasoned that my trip to see my parents was as critical at the time as the risk I was taking.

The journey to Nakuru and back was uneventful. And the baby held on. On my way to Murang'a, I decided to take as much food as I possibly could for my family, my parents were farmers. I also decided to pass by to see how my in-laws were faring and share some of the food-stuff. Suddenly, as soon as I alighted from the bus at Kabete, the labour pains began.

But I had to walk about one and a half kilometre in labour to reach home, hoping to get some help to get to hospital.

I did not expect to go through the experience I went through. To begin with, labour pains set on before I could familiarize myself with my new environment. This was my first visit to the place. Ignorant of the family customs in this locality, I didn't know whether, or not, as a daughter and sister in-law, I could enter into the house without being shown the proper room to be in such a condition. I was confused and overwhelmed by pain. So I decided to lie outside on the compound under the shade of a tree. I was hungry, tired and in too much pain. I tried to explain it to the people who were around at home, but perhaps they thought I was joking. Usually people tell me that I am normally quite brave, and my face rarely shows even when I am in pain. But the baby I came with was also hungry and tired and he started to cry. Both of us were helpless.

From 1:00 p.m. to 4:30 p.m. I was writhing in pain, and my small child was wailing. In my desperation, I began to fear I would die. Then Satan, I believe, took the opportunity to scare me further. I sensed some silent whisper, which told me this was my punishment for my disobedience. It said that now I would die and go to hell. But the agony I was going through could not allow me to pay much attention to Satan's threats for he did not give me any solution either. I continued to writhe in pain and to pull the grass where I lay until I uprooted it.

Finally, at about 4:30 p.m., I gave up hope and resigned myself waiting for the moment of death. Suddenly a family member who noticed I was in a critical condition notified the others. It was then that means of transport to take me to hospital was looked for. But by this time the birth process was at an advanced stage, and just five minutes into the twenty minutes journey to Kikuyu Hospital, the baby was born in the car. It was decided that "since God had helped me and the birth was `easy' there was no need to go to hospital". It was true that God had helped me through the ordeal. But knowing that there could be some adverse effects of the aftermath of a difficult birth, which would necessitate some precautionary measures, I insisted that I should be taken to hospital, but to no avail, I was overruled. I was too sick to argue so I gave up pursuing the idea.

From that day on, I swore never to forgive or forget that incident. I was very bitter, bitterness I shelved for a long time and found it extremely hard to deal with. It must have taken me ten years before I faced it squarely. I remember, even after I had known the Lord Jesus personally, though it was clear from the Word of God that bitterness was one of the things we are commanded to get rid of, yet it was one of the things I found too difficult to just get rid of. It required much more than my simple decision or verbal confession to deal with. Therefore, at this point in time and in the immediate future, I shelved my bitterness and continued to nurse it.

Meanwhile, I stayed with my in-laws for a week while someone was sent to inform my husband to come. He came immediately and brought the needed baby clothing and the relief and consolation I so much needed. He was overjoyed to see me with the new baby. But he had to go back for duty sooner than I wished. He wanted me to stay on at Kabete and get more help until I was strong enough, but for reasons I would not want to disclose here, I insisted that we go back to Murang'a together. He had no idea why and I had no courage to tell him, I simply held tightly onto him and refused any further persuasion to stay behind. He succumbed reluctantly.

Several years later when I had known the Lord and was involved in His service, I came to realise that the bitterness I had shelved and nursed had become a hindrance to my prayer life and ministry. The Holy Spirit had severally convicted me of it but I failed many times to overcome it. One day after praying and fasting about it, I invited the person I was bitter with to my house. I had set up dinner specifically in my bedroom, symbolically to revisit the long past but unforgotten incident. Then I opened my heart to the person concerned to offer my forgiveness and to request to be forgiven. It worked. I felt so relieved and so free. The person was also so surprised and so touched. Our relationship took a different turn after this and we became very good friends.

My second visit to Kabete, this time to stay, was made with fear and trepidation. Except that it was made with a firm resolution to achieve a certain goal - get training in some profitable skill, do some further private study in order to position myself better in the job market. That I believed was a good beginning to improve the living standards of my family, after which we would possibly move out from Kabete to our own place. I added a sewing machine to my goals to try and make clothes for sale, which I tried my hands on and it later yielded some little additional income for our daily needs.

While in Kabete I tried to settle down with a new determination in spite of the odds. But it was harder than I anticipated. To begin with, this was the first time the children and I were alone in a house. And, as if to insult us, almost every day I noticed dogs would start backing at 9:00 p.m. to announce that thieves had come. From the time we settled in Kabete, petty thieves coming at night and helping themselves to anything that was left outside was a common occurrence. There was this one night, for instance, when they pushed the window open and started pushing the wheels of my sewing machine with a stick. We shouted until neighbours came. This kind of invasion used to be so frequent it gave me sleepless nights and made it difficult for me to stay awake during the day.

Then another test came in raising the children. One child for a young mother is enough to cause headaches. But, when that headache is multiplied five times in a short span of time, one is not far from going nuts. I had five children in six years. In the course of that time it meant changing napkins for two children at the same time while carrying one inside my womb. As if this was not enough, every time one of them caught flu, the rest got it too. So there were many sleepless nights and I had to learn, through trial and error, some first aid for all kinds of ailments without necessarily going to hospital.

Not all diseases though, were treatable through my self-taught first aid. I remember once when two children contracted measles at the same time. I was heavy expecting my fifth child, and of course we had no car of our own to take them to hospital. They were so sick I thought they would die. The nearest hospital was Riruta. To get to the nearest bus stop, to board a bus to Riruta, I had to walk for four kilometers. To be able to take these children to hospital, I had to solve multiple problems. The first problem was which child to take first, because they were both so sick. Then, there was how to carry them both when I could hardly carry myself. Finally, who would be left with the other one at home - my older child was at this time staying with my mother.

In the end I took one of the sick ones to a neighbour's house about one kilometre away, carrying another on my back and the other on my shoulders. Then I took one to hospital and came back for the other later. That these children lived through that ordeal is a miracle. Today as I look at these children, now grown and in robust health, I know it is nothing short of a miracle. They are now adults, some with their own families and away from home. I have also come to appreciate God's overall plan for my life in their having come early in life, and be out of my care at this time, when the Lord needs my full attention for the frequent travels and such a demanding ministry as I have.

In my new home I came across a reality that I had never imagined I would face. As I have said before, food was scarce, and so was milk - my favourite drink. In my parents home I had always had plenty of food and we had cows to milk throughout the year. I had therefore not learned to economize or to ration food. My inexposure made me think that milk and food were readily available in every home. I had been so protected from want and this made me so naive. This time round in my new family, I was being forced by circumstances to buy one or two bottles of milk every day, and ration it for our children and for our tea. This was too difficult for me and often times I would cry with the children as they cried for milk.

My husband used to entrust me with all his salary and leave himself with only a little amount for his upkeep. Yet, in my ignorance and lack of experience, the money would run out before the end of the month. After that, only God knows how we survived. Luxuries, to us, some things you'd think are basic requirements for nutrition, were only in the dream world. Such things like meat came once at the end of the month when Richard came home. My son remembers this particular day, when dad brought home a piece of meat. After cutting it ready for cooking, I went out to pick some onion leaves from our small back yard garden. On coming back I found that one of our dogs had entered in my absence and helped itself with half the meat. I was so devastated, but I decided to cook the rest anyway. We thanked God and ate it, and none of us got sick from eating the meat. At least I had grown some pumpkins in our small garden, which produced a lot of cost-free food supplements.

Today I know all this experience was not a waste. As nasty as it seemed then, it opened my eyes and my mind to new insight and thinking. It led me to a courageous resolve to be somebody. I knew I had to come out of the dungeon of financial dilemma and suffering to a new phase of life and no one except myself would take the first step towards that phase. I knew also that the way out was not easy or cheap either, but I knew what it was; it was nothing short of a proper education. I began the long hard struggle of private study for secondary school certificate as well as enrol for secretarial and professional courses. I plunged into these with gusto.

CHAPTER FIVE

BACK WITH BOOKS

It is incredible that I managed to catch up from where I had left in education and achieved the goals I had set. With my new resolve, that nothing short of proper education could take me out of my distressing situation, I gave everything I had to education. This was in 1967. I look back to this period of time with wonder and reckon how God, in His mercy, helped me through it all and gave me unimaginable strength and courage. I knew very little about Him, but He was behind the scenes, working out a wonderful plan for my life, which He would soon reveal.

I scrutinized the secondary school syllabus and selected subjects from the Ordinary Level Certificate, commonly referred to as 'O' Level, that were available for private study. I pursued the studies by correspondence. I even attempted some subjects at Advanced Level Certificate 'A' Level. At the same time I joined evening classes for professional courses. I mustered every bit of energy and used every minute as if that meant life or death. At first I wanted to pursue accounts for my professional studies. I loved Mathematics and had performed very well in the subject in school. But on second thoughts, I realized it would take long to complete, so I settled for secretarial training.

Even though I had my mind so set and my determination so ripe, once again I had to deal with my old time financial snag - the budget. Apparently I had yet to learn the tactic, if ever it existed, of stretching the money my husband gave me for food and now, bus fare and college fees so that it could last a month. When I started the secretarial training, the same old problem followed me. I would pay the college fees all right, but by mid-month, I would not have enough money for bus fare. This interfered greatly with the training. At the end of the third month, my husband came home to a tearful and frustrated wife. Tears had by now become part of my way of life so he had to think of a solution. He considered the matter and decided to buy me a typewriter and a typing manual. We then agreed I would train myself at home.

You should have seen me during those days. I started all my studies at once. At this time, I was expecting my fourth child. The others, all babies still, were often pulling at my skirts, while another would be hanging on my back. Admittedly, to state the least it, it was a very difficult undertaking. But it had to be accomplished. So, I devised a simple plan for my days such that my housework would take the morning hours while I would focus my attention on studying during the afternoons. My afternoon studies usually continued to late nights. Of course it wasn't as simple as it sounds, for often I had to fight impending sleep which would threaten my concentration. I fought this through the harshest method - dipping my feet inside a basin full of cold water whenever I felt sleepy. I just had no option but to keep awake by even the ruthless means, because this was the only quiet time to concentrate much longer when children were in bed.

The birth of my fifth child and also the last in 1968 brought some interruptions to the tight study schedule. But soon after the birth, I resumed my studies with dogged drive, I had to pass and get a job, I told myself.

My thirst for education was insatiable. I continued with my academic studies and professional training. This took me about two years. Finally I attained the 'O' level standard. Now with my 'O level approved standards in the context of my professional pursuit, I felt confident and comfortable. I concentrated on professional subjects mainly in the area of administration whereby I attended several relevant courses. After three years of my private studies and professional training, my efforts were rewarded. Not only did I pass very well in all I attempted, but I got a job finally.

This however, did not stop there. Still, my thirst for higher education could not be satisfied. Even though I did not sit for A-level exams, I continued to study hard, in administration. I collected and studied papers that I believe were of University level. This was later confirmed to be so when I was seconded to Management training courses and found my self in the top list. Again my hard study was rewarded when in the1996, I attended the Haggai Institute (H.I) for Advanced Leadership training. I did quite well and was voted the Vale Victoria by the student body. Shortly afterward Haggai Institute requested me to join their faculty and I have since been one of their lecturers. The lord has blessed the ministry of H.I and while doing a video on "Making the Difference" they included my ministry to women. In 1994, I was selected among the 26 potential candidates invited back to H.I for further faculty training. This selection, I learnt, was based on personalities who were doing excellently in various ministries in the world. Upon completion of this training, I was awarded a special certificate, "Distinguished" member of the faculty team. With all this, I have come to the conclusion that we should never stop learning. But we should not allow certificates to be the stop-check for moving on! Acquired knowledge is an invaluable commodity and a wealth that cannot be equated with certificates.

When one is immersed into a thing so crucial in life, there is hardly time to think of the ripples and some of the effects such a pursuit may be having on others. I did not know, until later, that as I went through the struggles in life and as the Lord enabled me to achieve what I consider more than I anticipated, my children were watching and thank God, being motivated. Njeri, my daughter wrote about it in an essay at school when as students they were asked to write about the person who had influenced them most in life. Years later she gave me this story and I was moved to tears when I read it. She has allowed me to use the story in this book. I have done this, of course with some newer additions from her and editorial adjustments. I am delighted to share this story with the readers in the hope that it will inspire many.

What my mother gave to me

My mother is my hero. She is a very determined woman who sets her goals and achieves them against all odds. Her high sense of humour and her deep reverence for God have given her a character and personality very rare among women. She has gone through all kinds of problems and difficulties including financial, physical and emotional, yet she has shown anything can be conquered through faith in God and determination.

She grew up in a rural village. She gave birth to me at 17, which would look normal given the status of girls then and the prevailing circumstances of the day. My father was 25 at the time of my birth. With my mother's encouragement, both my parents enrolled in adult education by correspondence. Seven years later, with a family of five children, they studied privately and acquired their secondary school level of education. My mother became a secretary and my father an accountant.

While a majority of other Kenyan families in their circumstances would devote their meagre incomes to the exclusive education of their sons, my parents, despite their financial difficulties, educated all five of us. In retrospect, I know this was a very difficult time for my parents. I am indebted to them for going against the received norms of our society and valuing me as highly as my brothers. My mother's influence built in me a reliance on God, self confidence and a personal direction. I know this is why I have come this far in my education.

I wish I could say that there were teachers in my school who encouraged me to have some ambition for education, but there were none, unfortunately. All the teachers seemed to pay more attention to the boys in my class. Indeed most of my school male teachers did not regard girls' education highly. They advised me to become a secretary, but my mother counseled me against this, not that it was a bad career, but rather because it didn't require a very high academic level. She reminded me that, unlike herself, I did not have children to tie my progress in education down, and I should aim to be one of the most educated women in my country, for only then would I benefit myself, my family and other women in my country.

I followed my mother's counsel and, in 1984 I qualified for entry into the Nairobi University to pursue a Bachelor's degree in Social work. I graduated with First Class Honours. Out of 250 Sociology/Social work students, I was one of the only three who obtained the first class degree (the other two were males). Due to this excellent performance I was one of the five students awarded a scholarship to pursue a Master of Arts degree in Sociology at the University of Nairobi. By this time, my mother was deeply involved in ministry to women and her work was an eye opener to me of the difficulties women face in their day-to-day lives.

I therefore conducted a research project on **Impact of Marriage and Motherhood on University Female Students,** which investigated numerous factors that affect women's academic performance at the university. My mother gave me both moral and financial support. This M.A. thesis has generated substantial interest in the welfare of female students in Kenyan Universities. I completed my M.A. degree with an average grade 'A'.

After two years of working with adolescent and college girls outside of academia, I was invited to join the Department of Sociology at the University of Nairobi as a

Graduate Assistant. After one year in the department, I competed with the male colleagues and won the International Comperative Scholarship awarded by Indiana University, Sociology Department. I also won the Fulbright Travel grant, which enabled me to come to the U.S.A. to pursue my doctorate degree in Sociology. I have maintained a G.P.A of 3.80, including an (A+). I am the first in my cohort (of Sociology students, Indiana University) to complete the course-work requirements, succeed in qualifying examinations, defend my research proposal and to begin my field-work. Due to this performance, I was invited to become a member of PI Lambda Theta International Honour Society and Professional Association in Education.

In October 1995 I was awarded a Travel/Research grant which enabled me to travel to Kenya in 1996 to conduct a research on "Strategies for Prevention of Sexual Transmission of HIV among Secondary School Girls in Kenya". As I conducted my doctoral field-work in Kenya, my mother continued to be a major support of my work.

She travels a great deal all over the world, yet I know that she is continuously praying for me (and the entire family). She calls often, assuring me, and all of us of her love for us. I speak for all of us when I say that my mother has never neglected us in the name of the ministry. On the contrary, the ministry has expanded her as a person, thus enabling her to be a better mother to us. During her birthday, and on other occasions, each of us five children has had a chance to tell her from the bottom of our hearts, "YOU ARE THE BEST MOTHER IN THE WORLD".

****

Njeri's story is an eye opener to what could be happening to the children as they watch our lives and as they listen to what we say to them. I would not boast of this impact except in Christ, who made it all for good for these dear children, or else the whole thing might as well have been a disaster. I say this because I have known cases where mothers or fathers have pursued careers, or vocations or even ministries and as a result the families have been negatively affected or broken. However, it is only fair to say that it was not all rosy, especially because my children had to be subjected to hard work against their wish. As I worked so hard to raise my standard of education, I had to teach the children to be involved in domestic chores-boys as well as the girls. There was no question of whose role it was to either cook or clean dishes. All were assigned duties equally. This made it easier for the young house girl who was helping in taking care of the smaller children.

As every spare moment I had was spent with books, I had to cut off socializing and this was extended to the children as well. As would be expected, this had a negative impact on them, and our neighbours too. The neighbours thought we were too proud and private, which they talked about negatively. But as I look back, I see the whole programme, even though strict as it was, had a lot of merits. My children learnt and loved to study. To this day each of them is working towards improving his or her career. Njeri has told her story. Esther is doing accounts. Alex has just passed his exams for company secretary. The other two sons are studying for their Masters in Business Administration. My struggle with education became their example, that there is no end to learning. They did not like the discipline I subjected them to initially, but now they are enjoying the results

There are times when I look back and can hardly believe what I was able to do and to achieve in education, given the circumstances of the time. The energy that is produced in ones mental and physical faculties as a result of determination can make one achieve certain things that are unimaginable in normal circumstances. At that time I was busy struggling to further the level of my education, that seemed to be the case. I had not the slightest idea what the Great Master, the one who holds the key to all knowledge and wisdom was doing. But He was there, having seen the beginning to the end of it all, giving me the motivation and the strength, and working out His grand plan. It makes me marvel! How could I be so busy studying privately, attending evening classes, doing all sorts of exams and at the same time raising a bunch of young active children. Furthermore, how could I have managed so well when the life I was leading was economically and socially so stressful! But I went through it, I must add, successfully. I soon had to appreciate that God was working behind the scenes. He worked in such a way that He led me within that same period to discover Him. It was a discovery that made my life what it is today and one I have lived to appreciate and talk about. The initial news of that discovery, though something for me to celebrate, was, however, not very welcome news to the person closest to me. It was good for me, but I was to choose whether to keep it private or not.

CHAPTER SIX

KEEP IT PRIVATE

In our little village of Kabete was a church, which I used to attend regularly, for so I was brought up. From my childhood I had appreciated going to church, not only as a duty, but as a good habit. There is, however, this one Sunday in 1967, which brought a revolution to my way of thinking. What happened on that Sunday changed things so much that I no longer went to church to fulfill a duty or as a good habit any more. A special event was taking place in the church - there was to be a crusade for several days which had been announced earlier in the church.

In the village, life could be boring sometimes especially for ambitious upcoming professionals. Village church sermons were no better, they could be a real drag, at best boring. But whenever a special event took place in the village, even when it was a church event, many people got attracted to it, majority of them to satisfy their curiosity.

I was in attendance during this one Sunday evening during the special crusade. Unlike many usual Sunday services there was also a lot of singing and a special speaker was invited for the event. There was nothing spectacular about the guest speaker except that he was new to me and apart from his small features which would make him pass for a good village teacher - he was thin and well composed, there was nothing striking. Nonetheless, something about him struck me. When he spoke, he held my attention.

"Our reading today comes from the book of Ephesians Chapter Five Verse Fourteen," he said and read on aloud.

"...for it is light that makes everything visible. This is why it is said, `awake O! Sleeper, rise from the dead, and Christ will shine on you." This passage made the theme of this crusade. After the reading, which to me was as ordinary as any other routine in the church, the speaker began to expound on the passage and that is when something began to happen to me.

..."so many people were dead inside, yet their bodies continued to move. If your expectations have not been fulfilled, your dreams not realized, your plans not met, the shell of your body could be moving, but inside you are dead!" he said. He further went on to explain, "only Jesus would fulfill your life and give you peace by establishing His plan in you". He also stated that if one accepted Christ as Lord, one would rise above the circumstances. Soon I realized that though such words might sound ordinary to any ear, yet to me that time they came with such power and something gave freshness to them. I got quite amazed and my ears became quite attentive. As I listened, I knew what the preacher said made a lot of sense, this was no normal Sunday sermon to me.

That this was happening at a time when my life seemed upside down due to the pressure I was going through in my marriage, and the struggle I had to put up with was no accident. I believe God purposed that at such a time I would be more ready to listen and understand His plan of salvation and my need for His help. I began to reflect on my life, and as if in a movie flashback all my growing up experiences were brought into focus. I recalled my life history with such vividness that I could almost write it in the short time since the start of this crusade, to the time before its conclusion.

My parents were born again Christians. They faithfully took us to church every Sunday and I loved it. I was quite active in Sunday school and excelled in scripture memorization activities, which were common in Sunday school and I often won awards for it. I recalled as a child in Sunday school I had given my life to Jesus, not only once but several times.

Although in my little heart I believed I loved Jesus, this was more to please my Sunday school teachers and those who said they were saved like my parents, and, of course God. Those who had declared they were saved were then expected to give testimonies during the fellowship gatherings that used to take place often. I used to attend those fellowship gatherings and I would give my testimony. I was a small girl, therefore the adults used to lift me to a table so that I could be seen and heard by people. Much to their delight and pride, I just knew the right phrases and words in my mother tongue which would fit their expectations:

"I used to steal", I would say, of course lying to them. "Now Jesus has come into my heart, I have been immersed in the blood and have become completely clean." The adults would then rejoin with echoes of a common fellowship chorus in our mother tongue:

"Nitugukugoca Jesu,

Jesu Gaturume ka Ngai,

Thakame yaku iteragia,

Twakugoca mwathani."

"We praise you Jesus,

Jesus the lamb of God,

Your blood cleanses,

We praise you Lord."

This chorus was sung with both hands lifted and waving in the air. If, however, they felt your testimony was not 'good' enough and you could be holding something unconfessed they would sing another kind of chorus:

"Niuhuthite mehia ukona ta murata,

Muoyo waguuirio na gikuu kioneka,

Niukamenya mehia ti murata!"

"You are hiding sin, thinking it is your friend,

When eternal life will be given and eternal death experienced,

You will realise that sin is not your friend!"

This was sung with gloomy faces and a warning tone. My testimony was usually accepted. But after the whole show I would forget my testimony and continue with life as usual.

Pre-Salvation

Before this crusade, I had wondered many times before whether I should be saved or not, particularly whenever I experienced problems. Somehow I knew from my background that salvation would do me good, yet I doubted whether one could be genuinely saved. I practised a kind of nominal Christianity, though I feared and tried to obey God's commands. I also used to pray, though not regularly but somehow knew, through childhood experiences that God answered prayer.

For instance, not long after we had settled in Kabete, something scaring happened which made me decide to test whether God is real or not. It was at a time when I kept poultry at home. I had received a consignment of sawdust, which we piled in a heap outside our small house while waiting to empty and clean the poultry house before pouring it in. The booty of sawdust made an excellent playground for the children while it stayed outside. Hurling sawdust in the air and at one another was great fun. One day, a sewing needle accidentally fell into the sawdust and sank right in. This worried me to death. I did not know what to do. It was at just about that time that a lady died as a result of being pierced by a needle while sewing her clothes. The needle got stuck between the piece of cloth and the machine. She was trying to pull it by force when it broke and the sharp piece sunk inside her finger and straight to her bloodstream. She died immediately.

I feared greatly that one of my children would go through

the same fate. How could I stop them from playing there? And even if I tried to, perhaps they would slip out when I was not seeing them and go to the sawdust. Yet I tried all I could to keep the children from playing near the sawdust, but those with small children will agree with me that children like doing what they are told not to. Everyday became a nightmare for me. Which of the children would be pierced first? How could I see any of my children die? Then as if God was rebuking my folly that my fears and worries could neither save the children nor jerk out the needle, He gave me an experience that raised my faith in Him to a new level.

At that exact time when I was going through turmoil about the needle in the sawdust, I woke up one morning and while making my bed, I noticed a needle - right between the sheets where I had slept the whole night! I shuddered at its sight. How could this be? How did I survive the whole night turning and tossing in my bed without even a light prick? I couldn't help but ask, "What are you saying God? Are you saying you are even the God of needles too?"

There and then I gathered courage to pray. I went outside near the sawdust and faced it. My prayer was unusual and boldly said "Lord, if you really are there, if you hear prayer, and if you want me to accept you, let the needle in the sawdust come out." I was praying facing the heap of the sawdust. Immediately after that prayer, I walked straight into the middle of the sawdust heap and alas! To my greatest surprise, there was the needle. It kind of popped out and I picked it.

After this I had no doubt that God exists and He is there where He says He is. I believed He wanted to save me.

Husband or no husband

During the first day of the crusade, I felt the Spirit of God prompting me, sometimes wooing my heart, yet I felt that accepting Jesus would have serious implications. Firstly, I was just a few years married. My husband was young and handsome, and I thought he would not tolerate a 'saved' wife. Who would go out with him and in particular who would be his dancing partner? I was also aware of the other girlfriends that he had left in order to marry me. They would perhaps give anything to see me thrown away as a religious fanatic. So the first evening went by. I decided not to be saved.

The following day, I found myself at the crusade again. I felt so sad. I wished my circumstances were different, so that I would be free to get saved. I seemed to agree with the preacher that only Jesus could give a fulfilling life, but how would I accept Jesus knowing very well that chances of being kicked away from my home and marriage were many? So again the second evening went by without my making a decision. I would try to stand and accept the Lord when the final invitation was made, but something would whisper, "You stand, go forward, but that is the end of your marriage."

The tug of war went on undetected by either the preacher or the people around me. On the third evening, as I again sat in the meeting, the preacher went on expounding the same verse. He said, "The light of Jesus will shine on you, on your path and on your future." That did it! I thought to myself, for how long would I stand between two opinions? Then, I decided, husband or no husband, I would rather have the light of Jesus shining on me than anything else. So, at the conclusion of the meeting in August 1967, I stood up, went forward and accepted the Lord Jesus into my life.

Unlike when I was a little girl, this time I was conscious of what I was doing and not trying to be acceptable to the saved people. My resolve to be saved was also with the realization that I was taking a real risk on my marriage. I didn't know the full extent of the consequences but I knew there would be some. Nevertheless, something happened in my life. I experienced an instant change and a new unexplainable peace filled my heart. I also experienced unknown joy. Above all, I felt so clean and burden-free.

That evening, as I looked up at the sky, the moon was clear and the stars were bright. I thought I could almost see Jesus. As we walked home, I prayed, "Oh God, please take me home to heaven before I fall back into sin." I really meant it. "Lord, I feel so clean, so fresh. Please take me home, "He did not. That is why I am here, serving Him and writing this book. I have been given this opportunity to tell you this story and declare God's rich salvation through Jesus Christ to the lost on earth.

New Challenge

After salvation, then what? I began a new chapter in life. But this chapter had to begin with Richard my husband. Every day I wrote bits of a long letter to him. He was still working away from home. I told him I had accepted Jesus as my personal Saviour. I apologized for any inconvenience this may cause him and I said I hoped he would not find it impossible to stay married to a "saved" person. I finally mailed the letter.

The following week, I kept vigil waiting for his reply. I would imagine his letter arriving and try to hold my breath for fear of what he would say. When his letter finally came, I lost all energy to open it immediately. I did not know whether or not to pack my things before reading the letter, but I eventually gathered courage and read it.

My dear Judy,

Thank you for your letter... it started... I read through slowly waiting for a crucial sentence. Then it came,

I do not mind your getting saved as long as you keep it private.

I was so overjoyed that I started telling people how happy I was and why! In so doing I exposed what I shouldn't have. I failed instantly to keep it private. It was just impossible to keep private such an overwhelmingly precious story, the story of Jesus. His love and salvation for all of us shown through His death and resurrection were hardly private, and so is His story imprinted in the hearts and lives of those who accept Him. It was too good to hide. To this day, I am still telling this salvation story and still married to Richard, now for over thirty years and we are very much in love.

From the time I got saved, I knew the importance and benefit of reading the Bible for myself and with the children. Every evening I would gather them together to a family altar.

I would read a passage of scripture and then explain it

to them. We would then all pray, from the youngest to the oldest. This practice yielded beautiful fruit and at an early age each of them came to know and love the Lord. They experienced how the Lord answers prayer since I always shared with them the family needs. We would pray together and they saw God's answers to the specific prayers.

Answered Prayers

Answered prayer was not new to me. From the time I was growing, I saw my Christian parents praying and the joy of answered prayer. For example, during the emergency days in 1952, my dad was blacklisted, "wanted man" by the Mau-Mau, the Kikuyu anti-colonial guerilla movement. I was too young to understand the details but I was told it had something to do with taking an oath. As a Christian, he refused to take it because it had to do with drinking blood and eating raw meat. His Christian teaching could not allow him to do that so he was put on the Wanted List. Verbal messages were constantly sent to him saying his head was wanted for the preparation of the next oathing rites. He worked out a plan with the government security officer so that every evening he would go to the post, which was guarded by the government security personnel. As a family, we also had to pray for our security. When we could not sleep inside the house, we spent the nights in the maize fields. We too prayed that the Mau-Mau would not know where we were. In particular we prayed for my baby sister that she would not cry and cause attraction to our hiding place.

Those were very trying days for many Kenyans, especially those of my ethnic group, which led to the Mau

Mau revolt. Two groups existed - the pro and anti Mau-Mau. Both parties were very serious. I remember witnessing an incident where a man, who was said to be a Mau-Mau guerrilla, was tied to a colonial government vehicle and dragged along by a vehicle which was being driven at full speed! The man died such a miserable death! His body torn to pieces as it kept hitting the stones on the rough road. In another instance, I saw a woman being stripped naked and badly whipped for walking home after the curfew time which had been imposed. Everyone was supposed to be indoors by 6:00 p.m. This woman begged the askaris not to see her nakedness but rather give her a severe punishment hoping they would understand the traditional implication of seeing a woman who is a mother naked. She begged them to increase the punishment but "not see where you came from". But they were arrogant and brutal.

In those days, it was not uncommon to see a human head posted to a tree near the home of somebody suspected to be sympathizing with the colonial government or for being a Mau-Mau. My parents therefore prayed a lot and we saw the power of prayer every morning when we saw dad come home.

Prayers also raised my mother one time when she was very sick. I remember that she was expecting a baby in the late 1950's. I did not understand all the details but all I knew was that she was very sick. She was in hospital for a long time and many people prayed for her. My dad was very instrumental in motivating us and leading us in persistent prayer for mother. Eventually she came home, very frail, for she had lost the baby but after much prayer, she recovered.

Another time we also prayed for my dad who was very sick with a heart condition which the doctors said was not treatable. This condition had lingered on since 1954 forcing him to retire prematurely from his teaching career. Now it was so bad and he had to be hospitalized. The doctors said that if they operated on him, his chances of survival were very slim, so they told him to go home and just wait (for his death). Prayer was made on his behalf and the waiting went on for another 25 years! He died in 1990 full of years. He was eighty-six years old.

He kept telling us how during his illness God turned an awkward rumour into a blessing. The rumour had gone round that Mwalimu (teacher) Hosea had died. Relatives and neighbours then began streaming into our home to console my mother. The comforters and supposed mourners brought so much sugar the consignment lasted for a whole year! That was a blessing indeed.

With such examples of answered prayer, I knew that God heard and answered prayer, so I encouraged my children to pray. Our prayers were never vague but specific. If we had no food I told them "Pray for food". Somehow the Lord would provide us with food for that day. We prayed when they were sick; we prayed for one of them to stop stammering and we also prayed for another to stop thumb licking, which had persisted until the age of six. The Lord answered all those kinds of prayers graciously. We kept the family altar until the children grew up and finally left home to be on their own.

In reading the Bible, I came across many promises that I decided to appropriate. Some of them included - Romans chapter Eight verse 32, that I am "more than a conqueror." Deuteronomy 28 Verse 13, that I "shall be first and not last." Jeremiah 29 verse 11, which became one of my favourite verses, tells me that God's plan for me is good. But the verse I stood on was Philippians chapter four verse 13, that, "I can do all things through Christ who strengthens me." One time I decided in my heart that I was going to do exploits for Him, not knowing then that Daniel chapter 11 verse 32 also talks about God's people doing exploits.

The "New Tradition"

I would not say that life became a bed of roses immediately after salvation, neither has it become so, but I can testify that I had a lot of peace (I still have) even though, I had to face many new challenges. Having been saved in a rural church, most of the saved people there were old women, who did not care much about their attire as long as it was long enough to cover their knees. For me, as a young woman, married to a modern man, I cared a lot about how I looked. I did not have much money to buy many clothes, but the few I wore were carefully chosen.

After salvation, I started going for the mid-week prayer and fellowship services. Then I noticed that, whenever I tried to hug the sisters in the Lord, as was the custom among the saved people, they would pull-off. I wondered why. Later I asked one of the ladies about this attitude. She told me it was because I used to braid my hair. During this particular age of the Church, the saved women had to cut their hair as a rule which, they believed was biblical teaching. Talk about total surrender and sacrifice. But I loved my hair so much. How could I cut it? Doesn't even the Bible talk of hair being a woman's crown. How would I look like? Quite awkward, indeed. And would not my husband accuse me of fanaticism that he had already warned me about? Yet if that was a barrier between my Christian sisters and I, the hair had to go. So one evening I sadly had a hair cut. I thought I would now be well accepted but I still sensed some distance. I guessed, this time it had to do with my dresses. Though they covered my knees I think they wanted them a little longer, but nobody said anything about it.

This continued even when I started working. My conscience was made very sensitive to such issues regarding how I looked. Therefore in all good conscience, I could not braid my hair, not even in the evening when going to bed. I knew God saw me during the day and night, so I did not braid it either time. That made it very difficult to comb the following day. Yet I remembered two experiences that almost confirmed to me that it was wrong to braid my hair:

The first one took place when I was young and still living at home. My dad had told us it was wrong to wear trousers, mini-skirts, braid the hair or have earrings. One day, I decided to be mischievous and braided my hair. However, I had to cover my head very carefully lest my daddy became suspicious. Mother did not mind very much, but she could not raise her voice above dad's. This turned out to be my unlucky day. As I bent down to sweep the house, the headscarf fell off. As if by coincidence, at that precise moment, dad passed by where I was sweeping. I trembled under my feet. I almost collapsed. Then he just looked at me and I believe he realized that if he said anything I would collapse. So he simply passed by but his look was enough. My mischievous spirit was broken that day.

The second instance was a dream I had soon after salvation. I dreamt about the rapture. Jesus came in a convoy of buses. I was taken in one of the buses. But a cousin of mine who knew that I was saved but still used to braid my hair sent word to my bus to tell me to undo it before Jesus came into my bus. I pulled the braids off the skin. By the time Jesus got into my bus I had completely undone the hair. I qualified for heaven but painfully and badly bleeding from my head!

Those two instances seemed to confirm the old women's stories that one should not braid their hair. After salvation, I read what 1 Peter chapter 3 verse 3 says, "Your beauty should not come from outward adornment such as braided hair and the wearing of gold jewelry and fine clothes." This was, and I believe still is, usually misquoted with an emphasis of Do not... Often the simple exhortation is missed i.e. therefore, your outward beauty should not be the priority rather your inner self, your spirit being right with God, as in 1 Peter 3 verse 4. Again many emphasized on a part of this verse, primarily "braiding the hair" and ignored the aspect of "expensive clothes and wearing of jewelry" which are all mentioned in the passage.

As I keep growing and maturing in my Christian life, I have learnt the importance of searching the scriptures diligently. And in my teaching ministry I have made it a point to make all efforts through the power of the Holy Spirit to "rightly divide the Word." I believe these women were sincere, but nevertheless they erred in their interpretation of scripture, emphasizing more on outward appearance and loading onto themselves a burden of keeping rules and regulations and missed out on the liberty wherein Christ has set us free.

I mentioned earlier about coming across Biblical promises that I decided to appropriate. I have proved how true God's promises received by faith in Him are. But also with God's promises there are prerequisites for receiving them. God require,s above all, complete obedience. So my discovery about the promise of financial prosperity is based on this truth. This discovery came just on time when I had already succeeded in my struggle with private studies and got a job. I was beginning to have the joy of earning a good salary.

CHAPTER SEVEN

AT LAST AN OFFICE

In February 1970, I took a bus from Kabete to Nairobi City Centre for my first employment. I felt very happy and grateful to God. I was now able to type at a speed of 30 words per minute (w.p.m.) and to take shorthand at a speed of 70 w.p.m. I was invited for an interview in the Ministry of Finance (Treasury) as a Copy Typist and I passed. However, since I did not have the relevant certificates, I could only be employed as a Junior Copy Typist. I accepted the position seeing it as an opportunity for more training.

Just to see myself in the office brought me a lot of fulfillment and gave me a lot of confidence. I now realized that the Lord had honoured my efforts. My hard labour and sleepless nights were not in vain. So I decided to work even harder. When my fellow colleagues went out for lunch, I stayed in the office to read and also practice more on my typewriter. Nothing could stop me now.

However, at the end of the first month at work, when we went for salaries, I was so disappointed. I received only Kshs. 280, an equivalent of US$ 4.5 today. That was the equivalent of a casual worker's wage. I was told I could not earn the Kshs. 450 or US$ 8 that the qualified Copy Typists were earning because I did not have the right speeds to qualify me as a full Copy Typist. I was so ashamed taking the little pay that I waited until other casual workers left the Accountant's office then I went for my salary. At that moment I decided that was the last time I would take that meagre salary!

This meant working harder to better my professional status and income. It meant further adjustments to my family life. The children were still growing, yet so much of their quality of life depended on what I had to do then to improve their situation, and how I did it. Alex, my second born child and first son, somehow, became my right-hand man in this struggle. Many years later, he too remembers this experience and the impact my life had on him, which he has graciously agreed to share in this chapter...

About my mother

My early memories date back to my formative years when I was a very small boy. This is principally because, although I was the second born of the five children, our first born sister lived away from us with our grandparents. Consequently, I was given a lot of responsibilities. During those days, we did not have house help simply because we could not afford one. This meant that these duties were shared between my mother and myself. These included cooking, cleaning the house, taking care of the small babies who were by then three, and all the other chores in running a home with small children.

A typical day would start at about 5:00 a.m. for my

78

mother. She would wake me up to light the fire, while she prepared the foodstuff for breakfast and lunch of the day. She would then wake the three babies, wash them and feed them their breakfast. She would prepare their lunch and pack it in such a manner for me to be able to feed them while she was away to work - she did not have the time, means or resources to travel back home for lunch by public means.

In the evening, she would come home exhausted. However, as we were small, she would take time to clean the house, clean the nappies and prepare supper. She would then turn in very late to bed. As our father was working away from home then, she did not have the support of a comforter as she went along this very difficult period. But whenever dad came home at the end of the month, you could see the change in her.

She was very happy - indeed they were very happy together, they still are.

I had never heard her complain, at least she had a job and she could assist in supporting the family. Before she got the job, we lacked many essential things. She had to wait for dad to bring the money to buy food at the end of the month. As he didn't have a very well paying job, we could only afford basic necessities.

I vividly recall a day when dad surprised mother and I with a piece of meat (surprised because it wasn't the usual end of month). We were so excited about the meat as we cut it into small pieces to prepare it. However, someone called us outside for some urgent reason and we left the meat on a plate on the mud floor of our small kitchen. As fate would have it, a stray dog walked into the kitchen and started helping itself to the rare delicacy. By the time we returned, there were only a few left overs, but we cooked the left overs and ate with joy.

Against this background of hardship and loneliness, my mother came to discover God's love through Christ. She got saved. I remember she would take us to Sunday school in the morning, then to the main church service, to the afternoon fellowship and evening services. It was probably too much for us, but it reflected the fervour and vehemence with which she grasped her new - found faith. Soon she became Spirit-filled and the intensity of her love for God increased even more.

At this time she also embarked on private study and many times we would go to bed and leave her studying. This devotion was not in vain. God rewarded her and began to bless her as she got better and better jobs. Thus, by the time we were going through primary education, she could afford to assist dad to pay for good primary education. We all did well and went to some of the best high schools in the country. Further, we had moved into our own home with a number of luxuries like television, and my parents could now afford to employ a house-help.

As the Lord continued to bless her, she in return continued to devote more time and effort to doing God's work.

As children, she always read the Bible for us every day, including Sunday. This has left an indelible mark in our lives as we are all believers and have a fear for the things of God.

She went on to form Women Groups for praying for

families. I remember in the early days there were groups of two or three women praying at our home. Because of her diligence and faithfulness, this group has now grown into a mass movement of women praying for families.

She is also a member of various Women's Organisations, both local and international, where she is being used in leadership positions.

She is an excellent example of how God in His will can transform a woman as an instrument for His work. She embodies the truths in the Bible that, if we put God first, all other things will be added unto us.

God has blessed her in the last two years with two grandchildren named after her and a grand son. She is a continuous encouragement to us her children, to women and others all over the world and Christ's Church in general. We pray that she continues in the same spirit and that God will continue to strengthen and bless her even more.

****

As I worked hard towards improving my typing and secretarial skills, my speeds improved quite noticeably, so I booked for Pitman's typing exams. The intermediate examination was tougher and more demanding. One was expected not only to type but to tabulate, answer questions on office practice, and do an open-typing exam. Since I had not completed the secretarial training, I was not so sure of this exam. So, I borrowed past exam papers from my friends in the office and studied them thoroughly. To be on the safe side, I decided to book for exams for both the open speed 40 words per minute (w.p.m.) and the intermediate paper.

When the results came out a month later, I had passed the intermediate exams with first class honours! The Government policy then was that, if one passed any professional exam, there was an immediate promotion, with additional salary arrears back-dated to the day one passed the exam. Can you imagine my joy then when I went to the Accountants' office to collect my new salary, no longer as a casual but as a fully qualified copy typist!

This joy increased my resolve to improve my status, so I continued reading and also booked for shorthand exams. I would book for two exams together, just in case I failed in one. For example, I would book to take two shorthand exams one week after the other. I ended up getting two certificates for shorthand 80 words per minute, two for shorthand 100 words per minute and two for 120 words per minute. By the time I sat for the 120 words per minute shorthand test, I had improved so much that I was able to take shorthand at a speed of 180 w.p.m.

Then everything to me turned out to be shorthand. While sitting on a bus I would write in my mind the songs they were playing in shorthand, while sitting in a hotel to eat and while listening to the news - I would find myself turning everything around me into shorthand. Church was not spared either. If the sermon was not interesting, I would take it in shorthand. Oh! Everything was just shorthand, shorthand. I would even sit down in the evening at home to take the evening news in shorthand. That way my speed really improved. Within two years, I moved from a copy typist category to a full secretary. Every certificate gained meant a salary increment. This was too good to be true.

While enjoying my new progress in my profession and the financial rewards, I discovered a new secret in the Bible about financial blessings and prosperity.

Giving

Just about the time I started working in 1970, I started attending the St. Stephens Church, Jogoo Road, Nairobi. My husband had been transferred from Murang'a to Nairobi and we had moved from Kabete to join him. We lived near Jogoo Road, so I attended the nearest St. Stephens Anglican Church.

One Sunday morning I listened to the preacher's sermon based on Malachi 3:8. "Will a man rob God? Yet you rob me. But you ask, how do we rob you? In tithes and offerings." The Pastor that day said he would like to dwell on one word only - Test Me. As he went on to elaborate I learnt that from Genesis to Revelation the Bible talks of trusting God, yet this is the only passage in the Bible, where the people of God are allowed to test or prove Him. What are we to test Him on?

The Pastor said if we give God ten per cent of our income, He would open Heaven's doors and we would be greatly blessed. This impressed me a lot. So I decided to try it out. Right away from my first salary I gave a tithe of about Ksh. 20

One may think it is easy when you are earning this amount and seemingly giving so little tithe. But I agree with one Christian millionaire, Duane Logsdon who said in his book, *Lord, let me give you a million dollars,* that he would have found it very difficult to tithe his first million dollars had he not tithed his one and a half dollars. You better believe that when you are earning Ksh. 280 you need each and every one of those shillings! I did not find it easy to tithe the Ksh. 20 but I decided to take God at His word. Firstly because the bargain as expressed in the Bible was so good, and secondly because I was desperate. And I tell you it worked. My salary did not stagnate at Kshs. 280 per month. I was now full swing progressing in my career and subsequent salary increments.

Having acquired various secretarial certificates, I got promotion after promotion. From earning Ksh. 280, to Ksh. 2000 per month within a very short time, and Ksh. 2000 was indeed a lot of money in 1970. That was like an equivalent of US$ 500.at that time. I climbed the ladder from the junior, to senior, to very senior offices, eventually serving as Executive Secretary for very high level officials in the Ministry of Finance. I will never forget one day, while in one of those very senior offices, I picked the telephone to answer an incoming call. My heart missed a beat when I realized it was His Excellency, the late Mzee Jomo Kenyatta, the first President of the Republic of Kenya, on the line. "This is Jomo", he said, "Can I speak to Mheshimiwa (Honourable)...?" Quite an encounter, but that was only the beginning. I later got exposed to many more high ranking Government officials and did a lot of high level Public Relations work. Why was God giving exposure to me all this experience? I didn't know then. Now I look back with a grateful heart to God for it all.

God knew this was the most appropriate training ground and preparation for the ministry that He was to entrust me with in future.

Back to the subject of giving, I would like to share a few lessons that I learned.

1. The Bargain

You must keep your side of the bargain, otherwise God will use ways that you will not be happy with. For instance in the same book of Malachi chapter three verses ten and eleven, the Lord God says if we test Him in this area He will send us so many blessings that there won't be enough room for them. Also as a result of giving Him our tithes and offerings He will rebuke the devourer so that our crops (possessions) will not be destroyed. On the contrary, this implies. if we refuse to honour Him in this way His favour and protection is removed from us so that the devourer can have his way to devour the fruit of our labours.

I had been tithing for some time and life had become quite comfortable. We had now furnished our home fairly well, even bought a television, which was quite a luxury in those days. We were eating well and had meat on the table regularly. At that time, I told myself, I did not need to tithe any more. By then I was earning more than Ksh. 1000 per month so I reasoned to myself that the Ksh. 100 I was paying for tithes could be utilized differently.

I wish I knew then what it was to have God remove His favour from me, and as it were, have more than the tithe taken away. As soon as I stopped tithing things started falling apart at home. The house-girl who was at that time taking care of the children stole from us and ran away. The children got sick one after another to the extent

85

that one had to be admitted in Kenyatta National Hospital at the point of death. We almost lost him.

After three months, with streaming problems, I began to seek God in prayer. I felt there was no doubt something wrong between God and I. I did not take long to realize that it was the unpaid tithes. I repented and said I would pay. The Lord did not let me off that easily. He made it very clear that I had not only to pay the current tithe but also the backlog. With difficulty I paid, and things began to get better again.

Since God took me through that lesson, whatever happens, my cheque for tithe is always first.

2. Gross or Net?

People ask whether one should tithe gross or net? In 1986, I had opportunity to travel to Haggai Institute in Singapore for further training in Advanced Christian Leadership. While there, I got a copy of John Haggai's book - "Lead On". In it he explains that if the Governments of the day take the pay-as-you-earn (PAYE) tax before letting you receive it first and before you divide the income among your needs, how much more should we be faithful in giving our tithes to God? The word of God in Proverbs 3:9 admonishes us, and I believe it, that we should give to God the first fruit (the best) of our harvest (income).

3. Blessings in kind

Blessings of God are not always in money form. Today I do not often get salary increments as I used to, but I have seen God's blessings in other ways. He has blessed my children in many ways. We prayed through all their exams, and by God's grace they did well and secured good jobs. The greatest blessing of course is that they are saved.

Something far more important than anything a believing mother would wish for her children, an eternal investment. God can bless you with good health, good family, favour with authority, success in what you do and so forth. Some of His blessings are even to be preferred than money, many of them are not quantifiable, many do not come by just by chance, but they are so good, so precious many yearn to get them by any means possible. But be sure God says He will bless us when we are faithful; He does not fail.

4 . To the poor also

You can never out-give God. By nature I have a soft spot for the poor and needy. I started noticing so many needy people and my heart would go out to them starting with my gardener, whom I led to the Lord 25 years later. Sometimes it would be people I met in the streets. The Spirit of God would point out people that He wanted me to help. I would just feel compelled to do so, I still do. There was one very particular poor family that I almost adopted. One day the mother shared with me how they sometimes had water for dinner and the youngest baby would vomit. I started to give them whatever food I had. As a result, this family blessed me constantly and prayed for me. Although I did not give them so that they bless me, nevertheless, I realised the word of God says it is more blessed to give than to receive, I inherited the blessings.

By 1975 my husband had changed jobs and joined the Civil Service. We bought a car, and he went away to Maseno for his further training in accountancy. I used to drive the car to work, and since there were some neighbours who also worked in town, I used to give lifts to many people, who in turn were very grateful and blessed me. I also opened our home to many visitors, important or simple. Again the poor would often bless me.

I believe it is their blessings that opened a door for my first visit overseas in 1975. In 1974 the mother of my boss Mrs. Marshall from England visited her son in Kenya. I opened the doors of my home to her (incidentally, I did not feel uncomfortable because of my humble dwelling place, I just loved people and still do). Mrs. Marshall was so happy with this gesture of hospitality. As she left she said she would reciprocate the kindness by inviting me to her home in England. It sounded like one of those impossible dreams. Although life had improved drastically for us as a family, overseas holiday trips were quite out of our imaginations. In spite of this reality, I remembered and considered again the text that the Pastor had given us about testing God and took this opportunity try it.

I said, God I have been faithful in my tithes and in helping your people. Won't you give me this holiday overseas? He did it. In 1975 I had my first overseas trip. I spent a whole month with Mrs. Marshall. We had a very good time. We even drove to Scotland, where I saw snow for the first time in my life. This trip was like a springboard to many more. In 1978 I traveled to Israel. Since then I have traveled almost to all parts of the world in the service of the Lord - you can never out-give Him.

5. First Fruits

I learnt with time that tithing has many facets. You should not only tithe money, but the Bible talks about first fruits - time, money, real produce, etc.

6. For Love's sake

As you grow further in grace, you realize you should not give God just to receive back, but because you love Him.

The Lord continued to bless me in many ways and after eight years, I had climbed the highest level in the secretarial cadre, and I felt it was time to move on.

In 1977, I resigned from the Ministry of Finance and joined an Insurance Company. I was taken in as a Personal Assistant to the Financial Controller. The salary I got was quite attractive and after completing my probation I received a fat salary increment. It was so large I could not believe it. I kept the money in my drawer thinking that my boss would recall it and say it was a mistake to have given me so much. When he did not ask for the money for sometime, I went into his office and said, "that money that you gave..."before I finished the sentence he said " Judy, I know you deserve more than that, but do not worry, this is the first increment." I will look after your interests, so please accept the increment for now. He must have thought I had gone there to complain, he missed it, I had gone there to express my surprise, perhaps it was a mistake, I thought so at first. After his response I was so happy I forgot to say thank you. This was simply too overwhelming for me.

Between 1977 and 1984, my salary increments came by leaps and bounds. Every increment reminded me of God's goodness to me and I consequently increased the amount of my tithes. I also learned about gifts and offerings as in Malachi 3:8-10. So I started giving gifts to other Christian Ministries. The Lord made it very clear that my tithes should go to my Church. Many people differ in this, but for me it was clear that the storehouse is my church where I get my spiritual food. A store in normal circumstance is where you keep storage of physical food, so I felt that my spiritual house is where I get my spiritual food. I have since then continued to do this for the over 25 years that I have been in my local church.

Promotion beyond highest expectation

Due to my job position and placement I had many more opportunities to develop in my career, and attended many administrative courses locally and overseas. In 1984, I was promoted to the post of Administrative Manager in an Insurance firm. Then in 1986, the Lord opened a door for me to attend the Haggai Institute for Advanced Leadership Training. This training is geared towards the development of Christian Leaders who in turn should train and develop others locally for the extension of the Kingdom of God through evangelism. This training was extensive and one among the best that I had received so far in management. Their system of setting goals and objectives has been accepted and practised all over the world. They call it S M A R T (Specific-Measurable-Achievable-Realistic-Time-bound). After Haggai training, I continued attending other management training courses and reading a lot of materials on the subject.

I didn't expect that my promotion would be given such acclaim. The management surprised me with an elaborate announcement in the Company Magazine. It read:

The Chief Constable of Gloucester, E.P.G. White once said, 'If you give a woman an inch, she will park her car on it.'

At Last an Office

How many women do we know in a number of professions who were given a small opening and have gone ahead and used it advantageously and are now topnotch professionals in a number of occupations? Judy Mbugua is such a woman. She is today the company's Administration Officer. Mrs. Mbugua obtained her 'O' level education through studying by correspondence. She later did part-time training at Government Secretarial College in 1970 qualifying as a Secretary there. She has worked as a top Secretary for 14 years, most of which were spent with the Ministry of Finance.

After joining Minet ICDC in 1977, Mrs. Mbugua has risen through hard work and ambition from an Executive Secretary to her present post of Administrative Manager.

"The sky is the limit for me," she says, adding that she wants to rise even higher in the insurance industry which she says presents so many challenges for women. To the women of Kenya, Mrs. Mbugua says that they should never feel that certain jobs are meant only for men, 'I have never encountered any discrimination because of my sex,' she says. She adds,"I felt free and plunged into the so called men's field and I am happy with the choice I made." Mrs. Mbugua pays glowing tribute to her employers whom she says have given her every encouragement and support on her way up in the insurance industry.

Yes, they gave Judy an inch and she has parked her car on it. Minet News, 1984.

The administrative position was challenging. I was

responsible for many areas and I had several people reporting to me most of whom were men. Some accepted it but others did not find it easy to report to a woman. One man in particular found it so difficult to report to this 'particular woman' who, after all, had risen through the cadre from a secretary to a boss. The timely intervention of my immediate superior saved the day. He was told that if he found it difficult to respect a woman, he should not look at the skirts, but instead should respect the chair. From then on he co-operated and became a good friend.

With all the achievements, I felt like I had reached the peak of a mountain. The whole package was now very good. I was able to dress well, drive a good car and live reasonably well. So I decided to settle and serve in this permanent and pensionable good position. Little did I know that God's other plans for me were about to unfold!

Judy in 1962.

Judy in 1963.

1985 Judy at home relaxing.

1987 Mum and Dad Mr. and Mrs. Hosea Wainaina. Dad over 80 years in this picture.

The Mbuguas family. Left to right;
Alex, Robert, Njeri, Judy, Richard,
Njambi and Kahara at home in
Kabete -1989.

Judy and bishop
Crouch in USA 1985-
AGLOW meeting.

Judy Mbugua and
David Wilkerson of the
"CROSS AND THE
SWITCH BLADE"
1985 in U.S.A.
Attending AGLOW
meeting.

Judy and Everlyn Christensen The writer of "WHAT HAPPENS WHEN WOMEN PRAY" in U.S.A-1992 Attending Exco meeting of the Women Track of AD 2000.

Judy and Dr. Luis Bush Int. Director of AD 2000 in U.S.A 1992

Judy on ministry tour to Australia -1993 speaking at Uniting Church of Australia.

1993 Judy and late B.K. Kirya, Ministry of State, office of the President, Uganda. Judy had gone for PACWA Conference.

Judy and H.E President D. Arap Moi at the official opening of PACWA
September 1989.

Judy in S. Korea with
Dr. Lee the director Torch in
1995. Judy was a speaker at
GCOWE '95.

Judy and 1st lady of Uganda, Mrs Museveni at the Homecare Dinner.

Judy with EXCO members of C.W.C. Dorothy Ingrid and Neela Manasses in Germany, 1995.

98

Judy at Blue House (State-House) with 1st Lady of S. Korea Mrs. Kim in 1995, Judy was a speaker at GCOWE and was invited for lunch at the Blue House in her capacity as International Chair Person of AD 2000 Women Track.

1996 Judy and Otto in Holland she spoke to a crowd of 30,000 people.

Judy ministering to maasai women.1995

1995 Judy and June Vencer attending a conference on leadership at Silver Springs Hotel. Kenya.

Judy in Holland ready to make ministry tour with Otto.

Judy and Dr. Adeyemo attending seminar in Limuru conference Center 1995

Judy in Homecare Dinner-1993.

1997 Judy and Richard

Judy and her grand children, they are both named Shiro after her.

CHAPTER EIGHT

INTRODUCTION TO A PENTECOSTAL CHURCH

I believe the Lord started talking to me quite early in my life, but I did not understand fully what He was saying. When I was quite a young girl, I remember attending fellowship meetings and asking to be put on a high table, so that I could give my testimony. It seems clear now, and I believe, the Lord was preparing me to speak to large congregations. I did not, however, anticipate how long and hazardous the journey would be en-route.

After my conversion in 1967, I felt a real hunger and thirst for the things of God. I also felt the need to give myself to God's service. In 1972, I started attending Nairobi Pentecostal Church (NPC). This was another divine opportunity. Nobody invited me to NPC and I had not heard about Pentecostal churches. My parents were Presbyterians and my husband an Anglican. Those were the only churches that I had worshipped in. As it happened, I was driving from the office one evening. I was in no hurry to go home since it would be another evening without my husband - he was away in Maseno for one year. I saw a poster in the city centre announcing a crusade in the City Hall by a certain Rev. Alexander Tee, sponsored by NPC. I decided to attend.

It was not a significantly big crusade, compared with today's crusades in terms of numbers, but it was probably the best I have attended hitherto. There were probably 150 - 200 people. But the voice of Rev. Mervin Thomas, the pastor of NPC, as he led the praise and worship, and the teaching of Rev. Alexander Tee sounded as the voices of angels. The gospel was explained in such a simple but beautiful way. The presence of the Lord was so real that I felt as if these men of God were touching Him physically. This was a real heavenly experience for me.

However, there was one snag. In the middle of praise and worship, just when one began enjoying the praise and worship they would start speaking in "tongues". At that time I did not even know what it was. It was gibberish to me. They would raise up their hands, talk, talk and talk, raising their voices to a certain crescendo, then all of a sudden they would stop (just about the time I was ready to run away). Sometimes there was a "message in tongues" with interpretation.

I had never heard anything like this before, but I knew vaguely that the Bible had said something about false prophets in the last days according to my understanding, who would go speaking like angels and would deceive many. I did not even know whether my quotation was a correct Bible text or not, nor where the text could be found in the Bible. But I knew somehow, there was something to that effect.

So, everyday when they began acting funny, I would be ready to get out. But just as I was getting ready to sneak out they would become "normal" again, after which they would call out people with needs for prayer. I went forward to be prayed for several times for various needs. This went on for the whole week of the crusade, and at the end, Pastor Thomas invited people to join them at the "Christ is the Answer" NPC Church on Valley Road, Nairobi. I had never heard of, nor seen the Church. I decided to go "see". That was in 1972. Today I am still attending and I am a member of the same church!

Although previously in the crusade, I had been deeply blessed by the ministry of God's Word and the music ministry, nevertheless I was quite uncomfortable with their "tongues" business. I started praying and hoping that they would stop speaking in tongues, but later when I visited their church at NPC., it was even worse. I began to attend the church regularly and it took longer in this state of affairs - there were more messages in tongues, almost every Sunday - which made me continually uncomfortable. I loved the church and the people, especially Pastor Thomas, but there was no way I was going to continue with those "tongues" speakers. So I made a resolution to only continue until my husband finished his training, then after that we would go back to our Anglican Church.

During one of the worship services, the Pastor told the congregation to look up to the balcony, which we all did.

He asked them what they could see. They answered in unison, 'people'. I was the only odd one out and I shouted, 'I see cartons!' Then to my biggest shock the Pastor agreed with them. They did not only claim to see people, but that the 'people' they were seeing were "so many that some had only room for standing." They finally began to praise God for the 'people' they saw. What madness! Now I was becoming more than shocked, I was disgusted and annoyed. This was the height of hypocrisy and lying.

At the end of the service I went to the balcony to confirm that those were indeed cartons. Before Pastor Thomas finished greeting the people after the meeting I was "up in arms" waiting for him. I confronted him to his face and told him how disappointed I was with him, in spite of my great respect for him, for telling such blatant lies. I told him I had already gone upstairs and confirmed that what they called people were cartons and if he was willing he could come upstairs with me and double-check. I had endeavoured to be a truthful person in my life especially after conversion, but this was unbelievable, that a pastor would tell lies publicly.

If I had ever seen loving eyes, it was the eyes of Pastor Thomas as he looked at me straight into my eyes. His eyes were almost wet with tears. He said in the most loving voice,"Judy, there is something called the Eye of Faith. With it you look, see and call those things which are not, as if they are." This is what Abraham used to do as recorded in Romans chapter four. He said that the church was trusting God to fill the church, including the balcony. That is why they refused to see cartons and instead saw people.

At that time the church attendance was about 80 people

on Sunday and about 8 to 15 for prayer service. I was encouraged so much that I joined and continued with them and how I Praise the Lord! I have lived to see the church building extended more than five times. Then I witnessed the putting up of a new sanctuary in 1986, which now sits over 4,000 people, with several fellowship meetings every week. I have seen one Sunday service grow to four services in a day. I have seen the prayer meeting grow from eight people, when we used to sit round the front part of the sanctuary for the Tuesday Prayer meetings, to now, over 1,000 people attending every Tuesday.

By the time my husband returned, I had made up my mind to stay at N.P.C., but to pray that they would stop praying in 'tongues'. When he came, his main concern was not the 'tongues' but the distance. We lived about 14 kilometres from the church and between our home and NPC are so many churches. He did not see the sense of driving so far away for church service. He was also concerned about my driving alone for the evening service and Tuesday prayer meetings. I had come to the point where I did not want to miss any church service, so I prayed about my safety. I told my husband not to worry - the Lord would provide the petrol and safety. The devil wanted to discourage me so that I would stop going to church in the evenings.

One Tuesday, instead of going to the prayer meeting, my husband asked me to go visit his sister with him. As we were coming back, I was driving and my husband was sleeping on the back seat. On arrival home we were suddenly confronted by a gang of three, which was apparently waylaying me in order to snatch the car. They must have thought I was alone. Two of them came fast to me to snatch the car keys. I shouted so much my husband woke up. Then in a flash he got hold of one and hit him so hard his colleague ran away. The other one was hiding behind the gate. Since that time I have never experienced any more attacks. The thugs must have assumed I am always guarded, which I am by God's own angels.

Another thing that I prayed for was protection from having to stop on the way in the night because of punctures, since I could not change the tyres alone especially at night. The Lord honoured that request. I then gave myself wholeheartedly to the church, attending all the services and serving in as many areas as possible. After that I became a Sunday school teacher and an usher. I was also elected into different committees; the Hospital Visitation and Women Ministries. I served in these capacities for many years and experienced the joy of serving God.

However, when it came to fellowships, I always experienced a vacuum. The Pastor would call for couples fellowship, single mums and widows or youth meetings. I did not fit in any of these and therefore felt very lonely. I could not fit into the couples' fellowship because my husband had not given his heart to the Lord, and therefore would not join me. And of course I could not fit into the others, the widows or single parents.

At about this time, I read a book entitled "Do not waste your sorrows." I cannot even remember the author, but I remember the message. The book encouraged every Christian going through a hard time not to waste time sorrowing, but to take advantage of whatever the situation was to the glory of God.

I prayerfully decided to take advantage of my situation.

I looked for ladies whose husbands were not born again and who felt they had no forum to share their situations and pains so we could support one another. I called them for a fellowship meeting in my home one February in 1980. About 25 of them turned up and we had a wonderful time of prayer and encouragement through God's word. At the end of the meeting, the ladies decided we should continue with the fellowship every second Saturday of the month in different homes. We felt that our "status" in the church was unique - we were born again while our husbands were not. We not fit in the many ministries that the church had in the structure then, such as the Couples' fellowship, the Widows' fellowship, Single or Divorced parents. By quick scrutiny of the church population of women, it was quite clear that about half of women folk in the church consisted of those who are born again but their husbands were not. Thus, these meetings became an answer to many women's dilemma.

The meetings continued every second Saturday of the month, being hosted in different homes. It acquired the name Ladies Homecare Fellowship (LHF), and later the word Spiritual was added so the fellowship was Ladies Homecare Spiritual Fellowship (LHSF). I had been asked to become the chairperson of the fellowship. It was also agreed that the fellowship would be interdenominational and as much as possible not to try to copy any denominational mode of service but to lift the name of Jesus only.

The following month about 40 ladies gathered in a different home. Within six months, over 100 ladies were meeting to cry to God for their families and homes. The Lord blessed each meeting with His presence, demonstrated through the saving of souls, healing of bodies, restoration of broken homes, and many are the testimonies that I can share to the glory of God. It would be fitting here to share some of the blessings and miracles that were experienced in these meetings. For instance there was Zipora, (not her real name). We met when she came to church. She wanted to accept the Lord but she could not get rid of her drinking and smoking habits. These habits were so excessive that she and her husband had to separate. Although he too used to drink and smoke, he did not want his wife to outdo him.

I shared about the importance of salvation with Zipora. She accepted the Lord, but could not stop her smoking for some time. One day while in the church service, she opened her handbag to take out money for offering, a packet of cigarettes fell out. She was so embarrassed. I told her not to worry about it, that since she had accepted the Lord, He would sort out the rest of her habits. It is amazing how truly, within a short time the Lord sorted out the problem. He delivered her from both the smoking and drinking.

The next problem was how to reconcile with her husband. It happened that she was entitled to some alimony money that was due but her husband delayed depositing it in the bank. She came to the Ladies Fellowship and we prayed for her need. We also asked her to believe that it was possible for God to touch her husband and bring them back together. She thought that was impossible. Her husband was a soldier and she confessed he was as hard as any soldier. However, she decided to try.

She called him one day to ask for the alimony money.

110

God had gone before her and they had a "nice" conversation on telephone following which her husband asked her to go for the money personally. Sharing her testimony later, she said when she went, her husband asked her to spend the night, explaining to her that it was not necessary for her to go home so late at night. The next day she was asked to wait for a few days, and somehow she enjoyed the 'waiting' so much that she never went back. They are now together.

Another testimony is that of another woman. This lady's husband had disappeared from home and left her with little children. It had been fourteen years since.

She says in her testimony, "I could not remember how my husband looked like. Was he tall, short, fat or thin? We had been separated for fourteen years! My children were just little boys when their daddy left home and now they were men. How could any of us remember him? One day, I was in bed trying to sleep after a late night of drinking and the like."

"This particular night, sleep would just not come. As I lay there, very clearly as if it was in real life, I saw a vision, rather like a 'motion picture' I was shown all my sins from the time I was a small girl to the present. 'This vision set me to action', she says.

"Before this, some one had been witnessing to me to accept Jesus and for a while I had resisted. It was undoubtedly clear from the vision that I was known by God. As soon as I woke up I called the lady who had been witnessing to me to take me to church."

This woman was saved that day. She was later introduced to the Ladies Homecare Spiritual Fellowship. Then in one particular meeting, she says, "Judy Mbugua called us and admonished us to `ask God for the impossible.' In my heart I vowed to do just that. I said, `God, it is impossible to have my husband back, but we were told to ask you for the impossible, so I ask for him!' Some weeks later, I felt I should pray and fast. I decided to do that for seven days. On the eighth day, I went to have coffee in town with that same friend I had called to take me to church. As we were having tea, a mutual friend came into the coffee house and informed us that my husband was outside. I told her to call him in. He came in, greeted us and paid for our tea... We have not parted since that day! Now we are together as a family — reconciled!"

There was also this young girl, Nancy. She had dropped out of school in Form Two due to lack of school fees and had worked for a long time as a house girl. She had tried to save some money in order to start some kind of training. She could not save that money because her parents needed to be helped financially to raise a large family. LHSF heard of her plight and decided to help her. She was assisted to train as a dressmaker.

Later she had this to say in her testimony, "I thank God for LHSF because, though none of you knew me well, God found you and you helped me. I did not have a big brother but I have a big God. Now I am employed as a dressmaker and my life has changed."

The LHSF grew in strength and had been organized into a workable structure led by an executive committee. Within a year, over 200 women were meeting, and in 3 years, over 500 were meeting. We glorified God for the phenomenal growth. This was a great blessing, but it had its problems. Which home could accommodate 500 women? It was now practically impossible for any home to host over 500 women. We tried pitching tents outside the homes, but the numbers outgrew the space in the tents. We resolved to ask the church where I worshipped to allow us to use the church hall, which they readily agreed. That solved our immediate problem.

The meetings continued to grow from strength to strength and many souls were saved to the glory of God. In October 1985, we recorded the highest number of attendance - 1,050. The fellowship was made into a department of the church but we did not yet understand the implications of that move until later when some difficult problems arose. With this kind of growth, however, one had better anticipate for such problems. For instance, it had earlier been agreed that money offered during the fellowship meetings should be used to help needy women. Our earlier practice was spontaneous response to urgent needs. For instance if a lady came to the fellowship with urgent financial needs to get food, we would take a love offering and give her money for food. A good example is this lady who had asked that we pray for her because her children were getting so cold at night for they lacked a warm blanket. The only remaining blanket, was torn into pieces. The ladies decided to pray and act. Within a short time money was raised to buy blankets for the family.

In this new phase, the needs needed to be sorted out while the money was kept somewhere. Since the fellowship did not have its own bank account, the money had to be deposited to the church. When needs arose, and they arose very often, money was to be taken out of the church to meet them. For the ladies who did not belong to my church there were lots of bureaucratic problems. Ladies from other churches began to notice this anomaly and complained. It was also decided by the church administration that ladies from other denominations could not serve in the fellowship committee. This put me in an awkward position. There were also other problems that were not easily resolvable within this context. I was in a dilemma. At this point several of us decided to pray and after some time we felt the only way out was to register this fellowship as an interdenominational Christian Ministry so that women from other churches could feel they belonged. But there was one obvious difficult regarding registration. This was one of those unfavorable times in the country, the prevailing political climate was very tight regarding the Church and Christian Organisations. It was during that time that several Government leaders had made public statements saying that, no more church organizations should be registered. In all logical terms, this was the wrong timing to think of registering a Christian ministry. We decided to lay a "fleece" before the Lord about it. The reasoning was that, if the Fellowship was registered, it would just be a matter of reporting to the church and looking for a neutral venue for meetings. This was the first mistake we made- not telling the Pastor right from the beginning what we were doing. I would, however, hasten to add here that, keeping quiet about it was not a deliberate move to hide things from the church. But we thought that if the registration went through, then it would be appropriate to report the news. But if the registration did not go through, there would be nothing to share. I therefore felt that to lay a "fleece" was appropriate. That laid the basis for the registration of the Ministry.

Let me point out that this was not the very first time

women decided to gather and pray for their homes. Earlier, a group of other ladies had started a fellowship on Monday evenings and it did well for a while, but with time that hour did not turn out to be comfortable.

There was also another group that used to meet on Thursdays in one of the ladies' house. This lady later became the prayer Chairman of the Ladies Homecare Spiritual Fellowship (LHSF). I praise God for the efforts of each group. In all our endeavours, I felt such a deep conviction to do something specifically for the ladies, who felt lonely even among others.

By this time, though the fellowship meetings still emphasized the home, the participants were dynamic. We were not only catering for ladies with unsaved husbands but there were even those with saved ones, who felt there were many loved ones in their homes, either children, parents, and relatives who were not saved. The Lord gave us Acts 16:31 as the theme verse.

"Believe in the Lord Jesus and you will be saved - you and your household."

Even though we used to hold our meetings at my church, those who attended came from different churches in Nairobi. We constantly announced and clarified that our meetings were inter-denominational. Meanwhile, the official church Women Ministry was being held on a different day. Members of the church were free to go to both, which most of us did.

The work that God was doing in the LHSF and the kinds of testimonies that overflowed as a result brought me into a new sphere of responsibility. It called for a lot of counselling. I therefore spent a lot of time praying and counselling with the women. Coupled with my full-time job at the insurance firm, I kept very busy.

CHAPTER NINE

ENLARGING BORDERS

After some time it dawned on me that the Lord's call for me was to serve Him on full-time basis. As the fellowship continued to grow, I felt the need to resign and get into full time Christian service. I approached the LHSF ministry leadership, but they were not financially able at that point to take me on full-time basis.

In 1983, I was invited to attend the Women Aglow Conference in the United States of America. Little did I know this was to be the beginning of a multi-faceted and complex experience for me — of joy, pain, struggle and questions.

While in the USA, during one of the conference days, I was standing on the queue for coffee. I noticed an American lady looking at me curiously, and she seemed to want to talk to me, yet not quite at ease. After staring at me so keenly for some lengthy time, she must have gathered courage, for she finally spoke and said, "I have a message for you", I looked at her and wondered whether she was talking to someone near me. Then I noticed that she was addressing me directly.

She told me that the Lord had given her a message for me. That caught my attention because I always like to give attention to what the Lord is saying. After she gave me the message, I asked her when the Lord spoke to her and she said about a month ago. Then I told her flatly that the message could not be mine because a month ago, I was not even planning to be in the United States. I explained to her that even when I got an invitation later, it was very difficult to get a ticket and I eventually had to get one on credit. "The message therefore cannot be mine". I concluded for her.

But this lady insisted that the message was mine. "The Lord gave me your picture in a vision and as soon as you entered the meeting hall, the Lord said, "

'That's the lady. Give her the message. I obeyed the Lord so it is up to you to take the message or leave it," She said emphatically.

At this point I realized something was taking place. It was getting to a serious matter so I asked her to write the message down. She wrote it.

It read, "You are my chosen vessel. You are my royal priesthood. I have my hand upon your circumstances and I will not be moved. I will fight your fight. I will give you new life and you shall rejoice knowing that I am your source and I am your life."

I was a little astonished and wondered what kind of a message this was, hardly did I know what awaited me soon after. I came back excited after the conference and one of the exciting things I shared with the Fellowship's Executive Committee and the Church Leadership was that I was convinced it was time to get into full time ministry, and to give full commitment to the Homecare Fellowship. Unfortunately my excitement turned to sadness when the request was declined. The feeling of the church committee was, it was not yet time for me to get into full time ministry. The church also did not have funds to sponsor such a position. Homecare wanted me to start immediately, but they had no funds I was stunned. However, I decided to wait and pray. Trusting God would cause things to work in His own way one day.

Once again in 1985, I went to the United States of America for another Women's Aglow Conference. Prior to my departure, I felt the Lord leading me to have the Ladies Homecare Spiritual Fellowship ministry expanded to other parts of the country. As I was driving home alone after the church prayer meeting, I felt a clear distinct impression on my heart, that the Lord was speaking to me through the words of Isaiah. 54:2. "Enlarge the place of your tent, stretch your tent curtains wide, do not hold back; lengthen your cords, strengthen your stakes."

The thought of registering the LHF ministry and enlarging the border had come up many times earlier, but I had dismissed it. Yet there were pleas from other women believers in the fellowship outside Nairobi who desired that such a ministry should be taken to their vicinities. Even though those pleas and desires were genuine, I did not give the idea a serious thought. But when this impression came and held on to my heart and mind without giving me a break, I shared the idea with other sisters in the Lord who also saw the need for the ministry to be registered in order to give it a stronger base for expansion. Going by the diversity of denominational representation in this fellowship, I also saw the immediate need for such an endeavour. Women from other churches were unable to participate fully in this fellowship by virtue of the fellowship flourishing under the umbrella of NPC, there was no way they could be fully involved, especially in decision making.

CHAPTER TEN

THE CALL AND THE "REFINER'S FIRE"

Disappointment, disappointment, disappointment! What a disappointment! Those were the only words could utter on that day in December 1985. Across my desk was one of the men of God I loved and respected. He had come to deliver a letter telling me I could not start my new ministry for six months. I said to him, that did not agree with the great commission that says,"Go ye..." which to me sounded like 'go without delay!' There were other disappointments also — marital, financial, children and physical problems all around me. But the one that almost crushed my life was the one that I will share in this book. Men and women of God brought this. If I would give it a name, it is "false accusation". False accusation necessitated the writing of this letter. The false accusers were Christians. It would, perhaps have been easier, if the accusers were non-believers. The worst part of this accusation was because my efforts to have a Round Table meeting to discuss the matter and clear the air were disregarded. What was all this? My mind went back to the history of how this came to be!

The year 1985 is very significant to my life. It is a year marked by unique experiences related to my call to ministry. I began to have a very serious struggle. At the same time I had a very strong desire to confirm God's call and leading. I faced unprecedented hurdles and discouragement, in addition to a "wilderness" experience of doubts and fears. Some of the experiences were so significantly extraordinary that I decided to diligently keep a diary of records of events, impressions, thoughts, messages and any related issue on the matter so that I did not miss any of the steps the Lord would lead me through. I will, in the next chapter, share these as I recorded them, in order to encourage fellow Christians and God's servants, especially those struggling in the dark valley, praying and waiting for God's definite word and leading.

Since there were some fellow Christians involved in one way or another in this phase of my fiery preparation, I would want to state here that in no way do I intend to expose, judge, or offend them, or even jeopardize the church of Christ in this matter. I do, however, realize how hard it is to describe truthfully, events and happenings, without including the people surrounding them, since life is made up of people, events and things. I also realise how difficult it is to safeguard misunderstanding, so commonly incidental in print. Again, good intentions may not always concur with the effects of their expressions.

When we, human beings, are going through tough experiences, sometimes hard to understand, and seeking answers at such times without a breakthrough, it is easy to question God's dealings with us or to even give up. I have come to realize and accept the fact that the Lord in His sovereignty does what He wills and uses His own ways and channels to fulfill His purposes. It is through submitting to Him and waiting patiently for Him, that in due course, we come to understand better. For who can question His works? Who has been His counsellor? He asks, and tells us that His thoughts and His ways are higher than ours (Isaiah 55:8).

I believe God molds us and purifies us through different ways, such as circumstances (some very harsh), through people, sometimes even allowing some believers to add the fuel to the "fire", and also, through events. Through all this, God will "create" His own servants.

I had returned from the USA in 1985 after the Women Aglow Conference. At this time I had been pondering over the thought of registering the Ladies Homecare Fellowship when, in one church service, the Pastor came with a unique message that spoke to me. I was struck by his key statement in this message, that God had called him to "break" the church by asking each person who had a call from God to 'go' and obey God. At the time, this message was therefore saying to me - SEEK REGISTRATION.

I was not only sure of God's call, but I was also making every effort to obey Him and I needed clear guidance on this. I shared this idea with some people and got different responses. Some, for reasons best known to them, said they would be very hurt if I registered the Ladies Homecare Fellowship, while others for different reasons said that registration was the only way to move forward. Some in the latter group felt that since the fellowship was already an inter-denominational one, failure to register it would hamper its growth. On my part, I took a number of steps that I thought would be helpful in making a decision on the matter.

Preceding Events

I decided to draft a constitution. I brought together ladies that I considered gifted to be office bearers. All of them were very enthusiastic and said they would be more than ready to serve as office bearers. That gave me the stamina. I began to work on the constitution relentlessly until it was complete and I was satisfied with its contents. After that I went to seek the Lord in prayer. I decided, as I sought the Lord, that I would confirm His will by the following ways:

i. **A *"fleece"*:** I laid this before the Lord saying; if the fellowship was registered, I would know that it was His will for me and that He would open doors for full time ministry. I prayed "If you want us to register the ministry, give us favour with the Registrar's office as we take the constitution."

ii. **God's voice:** I asked a certain prayer partner to pray for and with me until she heard the voice of the Lord on the matter. On 7th June 1985 she wrote a simple note - "Go ahead."

iii. **God's will:** I went for fellowship where I asked fellow sisters in the Lord to pray so that I keep in God's perfect will. That evening as I was listening to a Christian broadcast I heard the speaker say, "blessed are those who hunger and thirst for righteousness..." This was quite appropriate for me then. The Lord confirmed in that message that the hunger and thirst I was experiencing were from Him.

iv. **Constitution:** 8th August 1985 was a big day in my life. I completed drafting the constitution and polished it. It had taken me a long time to do the constitution single-handedly, without any legal background to back me up. *If it is registered*, I promised myself, *I will share with the Pastor. If it is not registered, I will forget the whole idea of going into full-time ministry and continue with the normal Women's Fellowship at church.* Meanwhile I had requested some ladies in the church to continue to pray. I took the papers to the Registrar's office on 13th September 1985. Again as I left the Registrar's office, I told myself, *if registered, I would know it is a miracle, since it is the wrong time for registering Christian organisations.*

I will never forget the day, two months after submitting the constitution, when a call came from the Registrar of Societies telling me to go and collect the Certificate of Registration. My joy knew no bounds. Thus, the Ladies Homecare Spiritual Fellowship (LHSF) was registered.

I received the certificate of registration just a few days before my departure for my second trip to USA for another AGLOW meeting. Unfortunately due to the timing of my departure, I could not get an appropriate time to share the news with the church leadership. During the trip, I shared the news with some of the ladies who travelled with me to the USA and told them I would inform the church leadership once I returned. I did not expect the bombshell that awaited me on my return. Things seemingly fell apart. I got a call from a close friend that there was a story circulating that I had gone to the USA to raise funds using the fellowship as my ministry. Apparently one among the women I had gone with had called Nairobi from USA . The caller had said she had some very important information that had to be relayed to the church immediately. The information was,

"Judy has registered her own fellowship. Judy has raised lots of money for the fellowship, but she is using the Church fellowship to raise the money. With the money, she has already bought a car."

On my return to Nairobi the stories had spread all over the city. All the stories were different, each latter version of the story was worse than the previous one. I tried to explain myself to the church, but no one was willing to listen. I tried to ask the sisters who travelled with me to join me in seeing the Pastor and explain it myself, but nobody was willing to be involved. Oh, how it hurt!

The accusations continued. People looked at me with suspicion. Groups formed. Even those whom I loved doubted me. I tried to explain my side of the story, but very few people believed. They quoted the proverbial saying;"where there is smoke there is fire." One lady told me that one of their leaders had said "if Judy can do this who cannot."

I had never known that a heart could stand so much breakage. I felt like my heart had been reduced to hundreds of pieces. That the heart was still there was amazing.

I thought I had thousands of friends, but I could now count with my fingers those who remained loyal and faithful to me. Those were able to say, "Judy, even if you have fallen, we will pray you through to restoration." I thanked God so much for such true friends. Yet the stories did not subside. I would pass somewhere and look at people and faces would change immediately on seeing me.

The worst was still to come. I was given an order not to minister in the new Fellowship for six months, which was the content of the letter delivered to me by the man of God. Some friends this time told me to defy the order, but the Lord spoke to me about it and told me to obey that order. It was very difficult but I obeyed. This was one time in my life that I experienced the joy of obedience, because the lord has promised us His presence. This time I experienced His presence in very difficult circumstances. He became more than a Saviour. He became my companion, walking and talking with me and assuring me that I was His very own. At my worst moments the Lord would give me just the appropriate passage or verse in the Bible to encourage me. These are contained in my diary, which you will be reading in another chapter. The Lord kept on assuring me and sustaining me on a daily basis until the disappointments began to be truly His appointments. I prayed more and listened more.

Some days were quite hard with some very unpleasant words being said about me. At one point, when the testing became too much I decided to take my false accusers to the court of law, since the Church had refused to call us together. On that day, I was planning how to go about it, when I received a letter from a friend in the States who did not know what I was going through. The letter mentioned the suffering of Christ. How, in His most trying moments, He could have called 10,000 angels, but He did not. When He was falsely accused, He did not utter a word. How could I go on with my plans after this letter! I rested my case with the Higher Court and the result has been beautiful. Among other things He has given me a wider ministry than I would have ever expected, and He has dealt with my spirit.

I now know the devil wanted me disappointed and give up but God turned these disappointments to wonderful appointments. The Lord has taught me not to be bitter. Would I want to go through such disappointments again? No! But if the Lord allowed it, I know He would carry me through. To Him be all the glory. I have always prayed to be like Jesus. But I have also learnt that in order to be like Jesus, I must share in the fellowship of His suffering.

Back to the rumour. True, I had a new car, but God had blessed me with that car even before I left for USA in September 1985. As soon as I returned, I immediately went to see the church leadership. During our meeting I explained about my struggles in wanting to be in full - time ministry, the conviction of the calling, the "fleece" and the registration.

Whatever the intention of this caller, only God, who judges righteously the secrets of men, and searches the intentions and motives, knew. Now I was given a new task to prove my innocence, which had already been made very difficult.

On 23rd December 1985, I was called before a church sub-committee to be questioned on issues to do with my ministry. I was informed about the phone call from America by one of the ladies who had travelled with me and they also graciously offered me a chance to share my side of the story. I explained and assured them I had not been given any money. My story was quite consistent. I gave them references of all the places where I spoke and where I received any honorariums. I gave them contact addresses and permission to call or write those places.

Following this, I said I would like to request whether they felt the caller followed the laid down rules in Matthew 18: 15-17 "If your brother sins against you go and show him his fault, just between the two of you. If he listens to you, you have won your brother over. Verse 16, but if he will not listen, take one or two others along, so that every matter may be established by the testimony of two or three witnesses," Verse 17 - "If he refuses to listen to them, tell it to the church; and if he refuses to listen even to the church, treat him as you would a pagan or a tax collector."

On Friday 27th December 1985, the Lord answered my prayer and a church representative visited my husband and I, to say that they had checked all the information and felt I was speaking the truth.

That was, however, not the end of the matter. January 1986, was one of my saddest month and on eleventh of the same month my saddest day. In spite of all the discussions and assurance a decision was made. Part of the decision was that I hand over to the church's appointee, the leadership of the Ladies Homecare Fellowship ministry. I had been instructed and urged not to say anything about why I was handing over the ministry, or where I would go. The leadership also added that I should not attend the succeeding new meetings for six months.

I found this very hard and harsh, but the Lord, in the circumstances had also instructed me to obey absolutely. He had made me realize that this was of Him, it was His training and purification for me, and if I didn't obey, He would repeat the lesson. He gave me an example of a good teacher who would not promote a student, who failed an exam, to go to the next class. He would instead have the student repeat the class. In tears, I obliged to everything that I was told by the church leadership.

One day I stood in the church and handed over the leadership of the Homecare Fellowship. It was such a painful moment. I had never felt so isolated and betrayed. I, however, was confident and trusted that God, who knows and sees the heart of a man and its intentions, would one day vindicate me. I did not attend the meetings of the newly registered fellowship. (These meetings continued elsewhere, now as an interdenominational registered fellowship).

The preceding events were lessons for my future ministry. After that episode, I had endless telephone calls from different people who began to express angry reactions and disappointment. Some suggested that as a Kenya Citizen, I had the right and freedom of worship, and that if the Government registered the ministry, no church should stop me. However, I knew the Lord is above all. I chose to listen to Him first, and He spoke. He said to me that His government is executed through His church. He also warned me clearly about moving out of my local church and joining another. For if I did, He would make me repeat the lessons, even in the new church congregation where I would join.

The Lord had, in His own gracious way, enabled me to hand over the ministry and to attend all church services as well as the church's Women ministry meetings since I was not barred from attending these ones. He also gave me genuine friends who prayed for me and encouraged me to stand the test.

Throughout all this time, I was praying persistently, asking the Lord to show me whether I did the right thing or not in registering this ministry. I desperately wanted to know beyond any shadow of doubt whether I had trully heard from Him or not. This time I also witnessed a certain lady, who had earlier said she would never lead the Homecare Fellowship, take over the leadership. As I puzzled over this, the Lord consoled me with a verse in Job 20:4, "Surely you know how it has been from the old, ever since man was placed on the earth." That told me that man is untrustworthy.

Many people, out of sympathy for me kept urging me to leave my church and join another and the temptation to do so was evident, but the Lord would not let me do that. On my own part too, I had no reason to do so. I loved my church and I knew, as a mature Christian, if I was wrong in all this, the only spiritual cover and advice would eventually come from the church, the body of Christ, where I had worshipped Him and received my spiritual food.

On 7th December 1986, however, I began to experience some indifference in my heart about the church as well as some people. I did not have the enthusiasm any more. I was losing interest for the church. Further, I did not want to see some people whom I felt had been talking behind my back. One Sunday I decided to go to a different church with a friend and, while there, I felt so happy that I was inclined to commit my tithe there. Interestingly enough, I heard the voice of the Lord and His prompting so strong; "No, your tithe must go to Nairobi Pentecostal Church."

After the six months' interdiction elapsed, I joined the other sisters in the Ladies inter-denominational Fellowship. Within a short time the fellowship grew and spread so much so that it had its presence in most parts of Kenya, with branches in 12 towns. This was one of the wonders and blessings I had to witness to confirm God's presence and approval of it.

It is now twelve years and the Ministry has grown from strength to strength. Its significance and impact on families and individual women is undeniable. Today I can only say, may the Lord continue to grant favour to this ministry, which was conceived with a lot of tears. May it comfort, bless and lead many families to the Lord, may the name of our God be glorified. Psalms 126:6 consoles me as I ponder over this! "He who goes out weeping, carrying seed to sow, will return with songs of joy carrying sheaves with him". I know my reward in heaven is sure, for "God cannot forget our labour in Him," He says.

I learnt one important thing in my journey of faith and trials; that it is very important to know God intimately as an individual. Then in times of trials, pain and doubts, one can turn to Him for solace and answers, with full confidence that He will respond. In my diary I had endeavoured to record significant events that I believe God used to bring me to where I am today.

CHAPTER ELEVEN

OPEN THE DIARY

Introduction

I started sensing the call of God on my life in the late 1970's but it was not until 1982 when I felt that I should respond to that call fully.

I had seen the hand of God from 1980 after the inception of the Ladies Homecare Fellowship. There had been periods of trial and error but when I started leading the fellowship I saw the ministry richly get blessed. This caused me to see that the Lord wanted me to work with and amongst women.

As the Fellowship began to grow, I saw great opposition and was surprised that it even came from Christians, and particularly those that I considered great friends.

Quotes from the diary

<u>1983.</u> I felt a definite call to go to full time Christian service, but still was not sure whether it was my own desire or God's perfect will for my life. While in this state of

indecision, God opened a very special door for me to go to America, where He had already sent a prophetic word for me.

After my return I shared with my family who felt I would rather keep my employment in order to supplement the family income. I also felt the financial needs in the home were many, so why this senseless urge to go full-time?

I also shared with my Pastor who told me he would rather I continued working, adding that, it would also be wise to share with the Board, especially because I had asked the church to take me in as staff or give me financial support.

24th September 1984. Meeting with the Board:

1) I was asked to put my request in writing, which I did.

2) I was instructed not to put forward any requests to the ladies of Homecare Fellowship concerning personal support.

3) The Pastor asked me to check the following:

* Timing - He personally thought time was not ripe.

He also thought I should give the church some time to reorganise themselves in order to consider any request

* It was thought that I should give more attention to my family and was warned of many people who have gone to full-time ministry without being absolutely sure of the calling and have ended up regretting. Also that the rapid growth of the Ladies Homecare Fellowship was no indication of the calling - things that grow so fast sometimes also break very fast.

* Another member felt I should wait until my husband was born again.

Another felt my family would feel the loss of my salary and suffer.

Conclusion of that meeting:

a) I was advised to be very careful and not to give God any prior conditions i.e. financial, geographical location or any other. Therefore, if it was God calling me, He would open the doors easily.

b) That a call and surrounding circumstances should not be confused, and that they do not always go together.

c) I must separate the call from my ego, pride or financial gain.

d) To remember that the ladies I wanted to minister to had their own Pastors also.

Some Executive members of the Ladies Homecare Fellowship had accompanied me. They shared that they too had seen the need for a full-time worker in the Homecare Fellowship. One lady said we should pray for distribution of the burden like Moses to the 70 elders in Exodus chapter 18.

I left that meeting feeling very dejected. I cried a lot after that and asked the Lord to remove the burden since nobody seemed to understand me.

1984 was a year of indecision, waiting to serve the Lord on a full-time basis and yet waiting to obey the leadership. There were openings for me to serve in other ministries such as Women Aglow, but I kept feeling that my call was to families.

<u>Friday 2nd August 1985.</u> I received a message from two Ugandan sisters in the Lord who were praying for me. They said, after prayer they felt I should move from this land (office) into full-time ministry. They gave me Acts.7:7, Gen.15:13 and Exodus 3:12.

<u>Monday 5th August 1985.</u> I came to the office almost depressed. My daughter Susan had challenged me on the walk of faith according to Hebrews 11:6, "Without faith it is impossible to please God". She said I better determine whether I was called and not who would support me. If I determined I was called, then He who was calling me is faithful and would supply.

This situation put me in a real dilemma, a puzzle too complicated to solve. Again I started wondering whether I was called or not. Yet I had a problem accepting that I should stop and leave things as they were then. I felt there must be some light somewhere. Where that light was, was yet to be seen.

I telephoned a dear sister in the Lord, Jane Njeru, whom I valued so much in the faith, and whose counsel I had really come to respect. I shared my distress with her. She encouraged me greatly and assured me that she had no doubt about God calling me. Immediately after the telephone conversation, I received a foreign magazine along with some mail in my office. I did not know the sender, but it came from Zimbabwe. As I read the magazine I came across an article which said in part:

I want to examine the calling of God, because we are faced with tremendous challenges in our times and generation:

1.   If you cannot make it in the service of ordinary life, you are no good in the Kingdom of God either.

2.   This is how a call of God works. It suddenly falls on you. You may not know where it comes from but suddenly you have a conviction in your heart. God has spoken. He has laid a claim upon your life and you want to respond. God's call can do two things to you, depending on your response: If you follow the call you will be perfectly happy and satisfied. If you resist God's call, it makes you miserable. Jesus is still calling and He is still the Lord of the harvest.

3.   Many people are offended after their call because they think they should immediately succeed Billy Graham. God has no High School. But He does have a low school. Learn of Jesus who is lowly and meek of heart. Elisha followed Elijah and ministered unto Him. He helped him. He washed his dirty socks and underwear; he massaged his back and cooked the meals! He who wants to be biggest in the kingdom must be lowest.

We have inherited the commission and we must respond.

To say the least, that article had no small effect on me, whoever wrote it and to whom the writer intended the message, it was clear, this was the word of the Lord to me. The Holy Spirit directed the writer and the sender. No doubt there was something specific for me in the magazine.

Wednesday 7th August 1985. Sarah Timarwa, a prayer partner and a lawyer called me and asked why I was refusing to go to full-time ministry, stating further that it was " because of house rent". She explained that she had a vivid dream where I was refusing to go to full-time ministry until I could put up some houses for rental. I told her sure, it was my desire to build such houses, so that I would have "security". However, she encouraged me to go by faith and not by human security.

8th August 1985. The Lord spoke to me through the words of Phil. 1:9-10 - "And this is my prayer: that your love may abound more and more in knowledge and depth of insight, Verse 10, so that you may be able to discern what is best and may be pure and blameless until the day of Christ."

13th August 1985. *I have made a final decision to follow the Lord wherever he leads. I have decided to trust Him for my daily bread - 1st Kings 17:4. I am waiting for his directions to full-time service, but my mind is finally settled - I will go. Most likely, according to me, December 1986. However, anytime He says will be my time, whether earlier or later.*

21st November 1985. Returned from USA where I had been greatly blessed. But everything seemed to have fallen apart. The first phone call I received was from a friend who called to ask whether it was true that I had been collecting money overseas using the name of the Ladies Homecare Fellowship. Rumour had it that I had collected quite a substantial amount, I even bought a car. I did not worry about the allegation at that time, so I told my friend that it would be easy to prove whether the allegation was true or not. I had a log-book and a passport showing the exact dates of my travel and the date the car was bought, because it was bought locally before my travel.

28th November 1985. I received a phone call from another friend and prayer partner. I was told the issue was bigger than the car.

Afternoon same day, received a letter from Robert Schuller Ministries USA with these words "I have not been disobedient to the heavenly vision "Acts 26:19. My prayer - "Lord, may I not be disobedient though the tears may blur the vision."

Evening of 7th December 1985. There was a visiting preacher at NPC during the evening service which I attended. His message blessed me a great deal. On that same day I met another man, Japheth, who said he had a message for me from the Lord. I had not met this man personally. I had only seen him from a distance. As he explained to me later, he had missed me in the morning service and prayed that I attend the evening service. When he saw me he was very delighted. He then told me the message, which he said he had received in a vision. In the vision he was told the following:

1. I should not go into business. It would not prosper. The devil would corner me.

2. There were 3 ladies trying to destroy me. In the vision I was covering my face as these ladies hurled insults and called me names. This was the testing of my faith - could I stand? The ladies had provoked me into temper and I was so disturbed,
    but according to the message in Colossians 2:2, I was to love them. To let them touch God who has all the full riches of complete understanding in order that they may know the mystery of God.

3. There was a group I should be careful of, who had a religious influence but who deny the power of God.

4. The Lord was re-visiting my stand. He encouraged me to go to full-time ministry and not to fear.

15th December 1985. Another pastor called me and told me he was praying, and felt inclined to call and give this message:

"To do the work of God without fear. To know I am here for such a time as this. To know if I miss this opportunity, I would never get it again and the work the Lord intended to do through me would remain undone. Also, to know that the walk would be very lonely, but to persevere. This message was topped by the words in 2nd Timothy 4:16. "At my first defense, no one came to my support, but everyone deserted me. May it not be held against them."

20th December 1985. A sister in the Lord called me. She wanted to share a vision (dream) she had seen. In her vision she saw me in America wearing a yellow dress with black leaves falling. The Lord interpreted the dream to her to mean that there was somebody who was trying to smear me with a dirty thing. The Lord said there was going to be severe opposition against me, but that the Lord would fight my battles, so I should not worry. The plans must continue because it is not the end time yet.

The Lord would also be my source and would start paving the way, so I should not fear or give up, but to be busy and yield a bumper harvest, which must start with an explosion. My best friends would turn against me and try to reach the highest authorities, but He, the Lord, would never leave me.

23rd December 1985. Still undergoing the fiery trials and the rumours intensifying. Very broken during lunch hour. I asked the Lord to speak to me. He gave me a verse in Romans. 14:11-13 "That every knee will bow and every tongue confess to God - Each of us will give an account of themselves, - so we should stop judging and putting stumbling blocks or obstacles on our brother's way."

At 3:00 p.m. the same day, a certain pastor came to tell me he had been praying for me after he heard all the rumours. He gave me several passages in the Bible to assure me that God was going to use me. It helped me to know, as I read through one of the passages, the eleventh chapter of 2 Corinthians, that even the great servant of Christ, Paul, suffered similar setbacks. This pastor also gave a prophetic utterance that by the end of 1986, I would have left my employer for full-time ministry and that they would give me enough money for one year. This pastor's prophecy, however, did not come true. I am glad the Lord has spoken on the issue of prophecy. He warns us in His word that if a prophet comes to us, claiming to have been sent by God, and what he says does not come to pass, we should dismiss that prophet as not having heard from God.

11th January 1986. After handing over the leadership of the LHF fellowship, I was asked not to attend the successive Homecare Fellowship meetings for six months. I found this to be very hard but the Lord told me I had to obey absolutely. He gave the example of a good teacher who would not promote a student who failed. These were lessons for my future ministry. People began to call me and some advised me that as a Kenya citizen, I had the freedom of worship, and that if the Government registered the ministry, no church should deny me that constitutional right. However the Lord told me that His government is executed through his church. The struggle continued, but the Lord also gave me genuine friends who prayed for me to stand.

11th February 1986. I prayed, *Lord, I promised you I will never question your call after all you have done for me. However, if I have missed your perfect way, lead me back into your way. If you want me to change direction, please lead me into your ways of everlasting peace.*

14th February 1986. I shared my experiences with Dr. Tokunboh Adeyemo who assured me he was "standing in the gap" on my behalf, because he believed the Lord had called me.

24th February 1986. A friend called me and asked me to always speak the truth and stand on what is true and he asked me to read Prov.12.

18th March 1986. A fellow Christian lady called to say she had been praying for me, and had asked one elderly man of God to come and pray with me. The man turned out to be Pastor Dass of Chrisco Church. That touched me - that, such a Senior Pastor would come to my office, though he did not know me. Pastor Dass counselled me. He then prophesied and said that God would bless my Ministry greatly, but henceforth I should not tell all people about my "battle" plans. Some would sabotage them. He also told me to observe the following:

1. That my first loyalty be to Christ, and Him alone.

2. Never let souls in my care backslide because their blood would be required of me.

3. There is a place where we should make a contribution to the body of Christ i.e. all churches (locally and internationally) to bless them, if one has a gift that can bless the body of Christ widely it should be used widely.

4. Caution: Not to go out too quickly before the work of LHSF is settled again as well as for the women in the fellowship to gain confidence in me once again.

He concluded by saying that God would strengthen me "What you are going through now, is meant to make you more skillful. There are certain things that God will reveal to you but you should not reveal them to people. He will also give you a healing gift to complement your ministry. He is calling you at such a time such as this in this country as Esther of old. More so He will stand with you and strengthen you."

3rd April 1986. As surely as the word from the pastor who called me on 15th December 1985, it was on this day when I was struck by a deep loneliness. Two of the sisters who had stood with me up until this time pulled out saying that their church would not allow them to serve in the Ladies Homecare Spiritual Fellowship committee. However, by June the same year they came back.

12th April 1986. I was elected National Chairperson of Women's World Day of Prayer and asked to represent Kenya at the celebration in New York, U.S.A.

On this same day, a sister in the Lord came to my home to deliver what she said was a message from the Lord. She said I should not start LHSF, because the Lord does not like home meetings. That sounded contradictory to the numerous Bible examples in the New Testament where even house churches were a common phenomenon. With the Spirit of God testifying with my spirit, I refuted that message. After this incident I decided to go on a two-day complete fasting. I beseeched the Lord to remove any confusion.

After this I had a meeting with two of the sisters in the Lord - one who was involved in the earlier saga of opposition. I had opportunity to share my heart out and to forgive her.

29th April 1986. I was invited by a friend to go to

the Full Gospel Businessmen's Office to meet a certain lady, sister Smith. Initially I went there to be prayed for because I was unwell and needed healing. When she laid her hands on me she simply prophesied. She said,"the Lord will bless you and your ministry. He will cause you to prosper. He will open doors for you to speak with presidents, because He has called you". She also added, "those who had been slandering you, God will cause to fall backwards.

22nd June 1986. I left for Singapore. I had been selected to attend the Haggai Institute for Advanced Leadership Training. This was another of God's miracle. My employer gave me a full study leave with pay. While there and still praying about the ministry and concerning all the "messages" I had received, the Lord led me to read some verses in 2 Corinthians chapter eleven where Paul talks about going "through trials, perils, dangers and doubts. So I was able to see that every servant of God at times, has doubts. But they are the devil's weapon to discourage us. I also talked about these doubts to Adetova from Nigeria who had a ministry reaching out to Muslims. He said doubts are part of growing.

22nd July 1986. I returned home from Singapore, only to find Satan busy hurling attacks on the family. It was one thing after another and I felt pulled down again. I sought the Lord and He revealed to me what was going on as spiritual warfare. This was because Satan was furious with my decision to go ahead into full time ministry.

16th October 1986. The family was in real turmoil with various unusual problems, but since I had already known what the secret was for me; to become more valiant in the warfare, praying, I pressed on in faith. In the morning I received a letter from a friend in Kirinyaga, Kenya, asking me to read Isaiah 43.

At 11:00, the same day, Dr. Adeyemo called me and asked me to read 2nd Tim. 4:5 - Keep your head up above the circumstances. Both of them did not know what I was going through, but the Lord knew.

Six months of my interdiction are long over. I have now resumed attending the meetings of the registered Inter-denominational LHSF.

9th December 1986. We had planned for a LHSF dinner in a hotel. We now had our first LHSF dinner and it was such a success. Over 430 people attended the dinner meeting and two got saved. The success of the dinner was reported in the Daily Nation newspaper. Yet in my heart of hearts I felt "sad". I could not explain why.

19th December 1986. A friend and sister in the Lord, Norah Masime passed through my office and told me about some negative stories that were circulating. We prayed and the Lord gave us assurance through Isa.54:17. "No weapon forged against you shall prosper, and you will refute every tongue that accuses you. This is the heritage of the servants of the Lord, and this is their vindication from me, " declares the Lord.

16th January 1987. I had a wonderful prayer meeting with Hellen Mcmean in her house. She advised me to be very careful as I followed the Lord and never press my own way. She said the calling and anointing was very evident, but I needed to be very careful as a woman in the ministry.

20th January 1987. I talked and shared about my calling and the battles I was facing with Rev. Wilson

Mamboleo. He assured me that what I was going through was a new attack from the devil.

31st January 1987. I met with Rev. John Perkins from U.S.A. He said he was pleased with what I was doing and invited me to Destiny '87 in Atlanta Georgia USA to share my testimony.

8th March 1987. Hectic week with World Women Day of Prayer where I had interviews on BBC to be broadcast in Scotland, Brazil and Singapore.

13th March 1987. Some superstitious people say that 13th is a bad day. Not this one, I was called to the church and was informed that the board had carried out some investigations and were getting more and more convinced that my side of the story about the alleged fund-raising trip, and the car I bought was true.

15th March 1987. The lady who had made the call from America during the Women Aglow Conference finally came to pray with me. She owned up to having made the call but said she felt convinced that what she did was right. What bothered her was that she did not share with me that she had made the call. Albeit, she maintained that, "The Lord" asked her to call.

1987. Throughout this year, many Christian leaders especially ladies called or came to me and said they had been praying for me. Majority said they were happy that the Lord had exonerated me. Many were now proud to be associated with the ministry of LHSF and with me.

I have come to truly know that the saying is true that, God does not use a man or woman greatly unless he or she has been hurt deeply. I do not claim to have been used greatly, but I thank the Lord for allowing me the experience of going through the "fire" and "deep waters", and for seeing me through it all.

<u>22nd April 1987.</u> *I have decided once and for all never to leave my church and to always seek their prayers and blessing as I go out to different ministries.*

Today in my morning devotion I read this: "Forgetting Our Mistakes."

...some of us find it difficult not only to forget our sorrows but our mistakes. Doubtless, the past year has had its number of mistakes. Probably they hang threatening over our memories and exert adisheartening influence over us as we face the future. If we are not careful, the mistakes of the past can hang like chains about us, effectively hindering our progress. We are tempted to feel that we can never succeed because we have failed in the past.

Mistakes, however, may become a blessing, and past mistakes need not be only hindrances but may actually be a blessing. We GROW by making mistakes. Before the artist can put a Masterpiece on Canvas he must experience many failures due to 'mistakes'. Before the musician is able to thrill an audience with his talent, he must spend years making mistakes and correcting them. In every department of life there are years and years with little but mistakes, immaturities blunders, while preparing for beautiful noble work.

The exposition is taken from Jer.18:4. Note - first vessel, made of clay was marred in the hands of the potter. Was the potter baffled thereby? Did he give up or was the second vessel less beautiful and useful than the one he would have made if it had not been named? No, the second vessel made out of failure may be even better than the one originally attempted. Because the additional working on the clay renders it more pliable and more yielding, the second vessel may be even more honourable. God asks in Jeremiah 18:6, Can't I do the same. In this passage God asks, can't I do the same?

The Lord says He will return the years eaten by the locust the cankerworm and the caterpillar and the palmer-warm. Joel 2:25. Other past failures that God used later are:

- *Moses in Ex.3*

- *David in 2Sam. 12:51*

- *Jonah in Jonah 3*

- *Peter in Mark 16:7*

- *Thomas in John 20:27*

- *John Mark in 2nd Tim. 4:11*

All this encourages us to believe that the past, with its delinquencies need not tyrannize our lives. That failure, however inexcusable, need not be a permanent handicap and that God's grace is not exhausted by His first gifts, Jeremiah. 18:4 - SEE HE made another vessel.

The Lord has continued to encourage me by giving me such readings.

This same day Sammy Chemwey, a brother in the Lord and elder in our church came and shared with me that he had a very vivid dream of me speaking to a large continental gathering.

11th May 1987. I received a message from Tara, a friend in Sri-Lanka, saying: "The wicked had drawn out the sword, and have bent their bow, to cast down the poor and needy, and to slay such as of righteous conversation. Their sword shall enter into their own heart and their bows shall be broken.

17th May 1987. Praying and travailing, asking the Lord to lead me and not to allow me to fail. Then I read this message in my devotions - "if we are to obey God's call, we must make sure that we are not overly influenced by statements and criticisms of other people. We must develop a strong character so that, once we have made a decision in the light of the revelation of God, we will not easily be swayed away from our goal by what people say. We must develop a Christian character," (all underlining mine).

19th May 1987. I got a telephone call from U.S.A. by Ellis Elward of Destiny '97 confirming the invitation for me to go and speak at the conference.

7th July 1987. I met with Bedan Mbugua and the late Daniel Kamau, who had been sent by James Mageria and Macmillan Kiiru. They offered me the following advice:

To seek help in setting strategies for the ministry professionally, we must be accountable - that many ministries were falling apart because Christians were not being accountable.

They said they believed in the uniqueness of the ministry I was involved in and advised that we must always zero in on our vision and never duplicate others.

We must decide how the ministry was going to strengthen the church, because no ministry should ever conflict or compete with the church.

Priority - they advised that I check and know when the vision outgrows my capacity of leadership.

12th July 1987. I had a wonderful time at Destiny Conference. *It seems the prophecies have begun to be fulfilled and the Lord is opening doors.* While in Atlanta I was invited to go and preach at Maranatha Church in California. After the message, they decided that should I go to full-time ministry, they would underwrite my expenses for one year. When this happened they committed themselves to support me, however, they only managed to support me for about six months.

12th August 1987. On return to Kenya, the Association of Evangelicals of Africa and Madagascar (AEAM), now the Association of Evangelicals in Africa (AEA), invited me to their 5th General Assembly that was taking place in Zambia. Since I had already taken my annual leave, I declined. However, I had learnt to trust the Lord for every step I took, so I decided to pray. After prayer I laid another "fleece" to the Lord and said - "Lord if you really want me to go, let me get leave from the office."

CHAPTER TWELVE

THE PLAN UNFOLDS

After the "fleece" it had now become clearer that I should go to Zambia. The Lord had given me the first affirmation. I was granted leave from my office but without pay. To some extent, this affected my financial situation quite significantly, yet I felt the Lord wanted me to go. Little did I know that this was the key to open the door to answering my prayer of over eight years. Then I realized getting leave even without pay was good enough.

I was to travel to Zambia in August 1987. I was now openly sharing about my decision to resign my job and go into full-time ministry with the Ladies Homecare Spiritual Fellowship. I shared about this also to a respected church leader. By this time people had restored their confidence in me. I had also resolved not to leave my church and to continue serving there as need arose. I was experiencing peace about it all.

The Lord opened a door for me to meet and talk personally to Dr. Bill Bright, the founder and President of Campus Crusade for Christ on 4th September 1987. He was speaking in one conference. He admonished us in several areas of our Christian walk and ministry, and in particular, for me, I was touched by the area of the attitude I should have when God is using others. "Never be jealous when the Lord is blessing another Christian group or leader (John.17) There is something wrong with your spirit if you do, because the Great Commission demands that we ALL GO. Therefore, the more people who go, the better, because more people get to hear the word", he said. He also emphasized the importance of working in harmony with local churches, never to organize things that would be in conflict with the ongoing church programmes or meetings. This helped me a great deal, to recognize and appreciate the overall plan of God in different Christian ministries.

On 2nd February 1988. I took time in my office to pray with Dr. Mae Reggy, a fellow sister in the Lord and church colleague. After a time of prayer and waiting, Mae spoke in a prophecy and said,"Go Judy, go, without looking back".

Soon after, I went to Zambia to attend the AEAM General Assembly. This was my first time to go to any African country outside my own, Kenya. During the Assembly, I came to know about the historical background of AEAM and its developments. Coinciding with this Assembly was the point in time in the organisation's phase of development to establish a commission that would deal with women affairs.

To initiate this commission, AEAM invited Evangelical women leaders from all over Africa who would discuss and agree on the objective of such a women's commission and the methods of carrying out its objectives. About 26 women leaders were able to attend. During the business meetings, the women were requested to meet on their own. This was a deliberate decision made by AEAM Executive Committee to allow the women the freedom to meet and discuss their issues alone without pressure from any man or the host organisation.

The 26 women requested me to be the chairperson of their deliberations. This was most unexpected on my part. I looked across the meeting hall and saw all the women leaders, most of whose backgrounds I knew. I felt very small. Therefore, I declined the request. However, they persisted. I eventually agreed to chair the meetings but on condition that it would be so only while in Zambia.

I knew the heaviness of the load of my office work back in Nairobi. Further, I knew I would need every minute to concentrate and compensate my absence, since according to my boss, I had taken time out to do "religious things".

The women were thankful to AEAM for considering setting up such a Desk, describing the action as overdue. For some days the meeting worked on the three main agenda successfully, which were:-To give a name to the commission. To chose the theme. And finally, to elect the chairperson to the commission's Executive Committee. My name came up again for the chairperson, which I resisted unsuccessfully. This responsibility had a lot to to go with it that did not favuor my job situation. I knew it would put me in an awkward position with my employer because of the frequency of time off it required to accomplish the responsibilities. The women, however, resolved that the whole Executive Committee would be responsible for the work. That gave me a little consolation.

We were through with the name for the commission; the Pan African Christian Women Alliance (PACWA), the theme; Our Time has Come (taken from John 17:2) and now, the Chairperson. It was time now to deliberate on the way forward. We came up with the plan to map out a major conference to launch PACWA.

The Nairobi Executive Comitee

On returning to Nairobi, I almost became part of AEAM. For one whole year we worked towards the planning of the continental meeting to be convened by the end of 1988. However, we came to realize at the beginning of that same year, in spite of the tireless efforts and labour we had put towards the holding of a continental meeting, it was quite impractical to hold it then. All wisdom and circumstances dictated otherwise. Our greatest frustration was in the area of communication. In some countries, letters were received 3 months after the date of mailing. We finally came up with a decision, to first hold pre-PACWA awareness seminars, covering each of the seven regions in both Francophone and Anglophone Africa. This would be followed by a major continental conference mapped for August 1989.

You can guess the implication of this grand plan on my time and responsibility, as the Chairperson. One was that, this increased my travel on behalf of PACWA to the various regions, including handling a lot of correspondence. It goes without saying that, I was holding two full-time jobs, for two years, without a conscious plan or choice. And for those two years, my mind literally moved to PACWA. My physical body was still at my Insurance Office, but all my free time and evenings were spent thinking, deliberating or doing work for PACWA. It was not a burden in my heart though, since I was all along, aware that my conviction and calling was to serve the Lord among women. And this was a joyful undertaking for me, and a worthy service for the Lord. I didn't know, however, where this road would lead to.

I put in my best foot to the task. I wanted us to have the best continental meeting, without the men, and discount the prevailing mentality among men that women cannot plan something well. This was not just a personal pride. I knew God's mind about women was not what most men had in their minds about women. I had examples in the Bible where God used women to accomplish great purposes for Him. I also had the personal conviction that the Lord was raising women in our day to do exploits for Him.

I was fully convinced, with good evidence, that the Lord was the one behind PACWA and He had a special plan and purpose for this ministry. I longed to see the success of the conference and worked very hard, using my time and energy, and even personal money at times. I had not the slightest imagination that, apart from giving my talents and energy for its foundation, there was any further responsibility requiring major involvement from my side. I believed in my heart that I should lay a good foundation for the person who would later become the leader, whoever that person would be. To me at that time, PACWA was simply a wonderful ministry, in which I enjoyed serving on a voluntary basis and doing the work of a forerunner.

How I dreamed with anticipation about the spiritual impact this ministry would have on the continent. I thought of the power of God raising the women in Africa to counteract the deception of the Women Lib too and that gave me such an excitement. In the meantime, I was still determined to resign from my job by December 1987, having concluded in my mind that I would go to serve in the Ladies Homecare Spiritual Fellowship.

The response of the different church leaders and other Christians around about PACWA was very encouraging. It was also clear from the commitment and dedication of the women serving with me that every step of it had the Lord's hand of approval. The women who served in the Executive Committee, many of whom were busy senior executives, in their respective jobs, made time for every responsibility they were assigned in the PACWA planning, all voluntarily. They were all convinced that the Lord was doing something new in Africa, and using them.

December 1987 came and went. I had resolved to tender my resignation but much as I tried to write the letter, I could not. However, I was so busy with PACWA work and there was so much to do that time seemed to just fly by.

As time went by, my situation was becoming more complicated. There was need to travel on behalf of PACWA for Pre-PACWA regional meetings, and it was becoming impossible to keep getting leave from my office. In April 1988 I decided to fast and pray, asking the Lord to show me what to do. I needed to travel to Zimbabwe on behalf of PACWA. Although I was due for my annual leave, yet I did not know how to approach my boss about it.

I thought two days of fasting was not enough, so I took advantage one of a four day retreat organized by one of the church's focused group ministry, the Varsity Career and College Fellowship (VCCF) at Kanamai, in Mombasa. I had planned to go and just spend the four days with the Lord. In my prayers I had asked the Lord to make things very clear for me at this point in time. This had further been precipitated by a talk I had with Dr. Adeyemo, the General Secretary of AEA. He had asked me to pray and consider joining AEA to be in the Women's Department, but subject to the Lord speaking clearly to both of us. I had declined.

In spite of what I thought was the immediate ministry placement among women upon my resignation, I had also this struggle concerning my level of education. Perhaps this had been exposed more as a result of my frequent interactions with highly educated people who apparently seemed to be in the high leadership cadre. This reality was hanging on me for a long time. It made me decline almost spontaneously, whenever I was approached to take up any high level responsibility. I rarely told anybody why, but when Dr. Adeyemo approached me about this, I told him I was afraid I didn't have a University degree.

I had received up to then, a lot of training in management and leadership, locally and overseas, and had a lot of experience. However, the devil seemed to have succeeded then in convincing me how impossible it was without a degree to rise up to some particular positions. He would keep whispering this fact, *no university degree*. At that time I had about 20 years working experience, and a proven record of what the Lord had enabled me to do in Homecare Fellowship, yet this secret struggle!

Kanamai 1988

I went to Kanamai with one resolve. Like Jacob of old, I cried; "Lord, I will not leave unless you bless me". During that retreat, the truth of Psalms 42: 1-2 came home in my heart like it had never before, "As the deer pants for the streams of water, so my soul pants for you, O God. Verse 2. My soul thirsts for God; for the living God. When can I go and meet with God?"

On the Good Friday afternoon, my Pastor, Dennis White spoke on the topic - "God is a speaking God". Later I approached him and his wife in their cottage and shared with them about my heart's greatest desire; to do God's will, and yet in spite of having said `yes' six years earlier, no door seemed to have clearly been opened for me. During our discussion, I shared with them about my deeper desire, that God would speak audibly to me, because I really wanted to please Him and feared making any mistake. The Pastor then reminded me of his afternoon message that day that "God is a speaking God", and if only I could hold on to that and trust, He would surely speak to me. All this happened outside the White's cottage. Apart from the three of us, nobody else knew my struggles or my desire. Even to the Whites, I did not elaborate what I was exactly struggling with, I just said I wanted to hear God's voice.

In the evening service, the usual programme picked up starting with praise and worship. At the peak of it, the unexpected happened. There was silence, then a certain young lady, sister Lucy, began to speak in tongues, after which she also interpreted. But she seemed to be struggling so much in her spirit and weeping in the process. Then she spoke and said; "It is about Judy. This message concerns Judy! "She could not even call my name out well, She was choked with tears. My heart almost stopped. It began to beat loudly. Then I began quietly to plead with the Lord, almost in disappointment and fear, *Lord! What have I done now? Why can't you speak to me directly? Do I deserve this exposure, that you have to tell everybody in this retreat about me? Lord, see my children out here - how can you expose me in their presence?*

Like all human beings in such a situation, I imagined all my failures and secret thoughts being exposed to the hearing of every one who was in that retreat. I imagined the Lord was now going to do that, and I didn't know how that was going to affect all and me. Lucy continued.

"I have My MINISTRY, a Women's ministry of which Auntie Judy is to head. I have made it public so that everybody knows it is My MINISTRY, and not hers, and also that when the hard times come, for they will surely come, she must not be moved, for I am in control."

At this juncture my heart settled a bit, but not fully yet. I was more curious to know how this came about to her and why she was struggling and weeping. Perhaps whether she had any more details she kept to herself. So I later went to her and asked her about it. She was open to explain her experience. In her own words this is what she said to me:

"My first reaction, yes, reaction it was! But Lord, there is the Homecare Spiritual Fellowship, and Lord, nobody will take it seriously. But even if it is another ministry, how do I know it will come to pass? Suppose it is my flesh and

I am imagining all this. It will be disastrous and then, I will have spoken in public. Lord, please let me go and tell Judy in her room after the meeting. But the Lord insisted that I had to speak publicly and standing in front of everybody. Finally, I stopped to struggle and prayed and asked the Lord to let me know if it was really He saying so. I knew the Lord had spoken. Was I to obey or not? I once again developed cold feet, went to the back of the chapel where Pastor White was now praying and shared this with him. I thank God for Pastor White. He encouraged me to follow God's direction and advised me to go up in front and share the message and he would be praying for me. So I passed on the message, and what a glorious moment it was for me, for surely God had spoken!"

At the close of the meeting I got an opportunity to share on this issue. I told them how, for a number of years, I had been struggling with this issue, and how I purposely came to the retreat to seek God on the matter. I expressed how grateful I was to God because in His wisdom He revealed this in the presence of my friends, my blood children, and above all the two men I respected most in the Lord - Pastor White and Dr. Adeyemo. Pastor White then called me up in front and explained to the people that there was now the need to pray for me so as to " separate me for the ministry."

It was on 12th April 1988, I was prayed for and commissioned to go to the Women Ministry the Lord wanted me to serve. After the conclusion of the retreat, when everyone left, I took another week in Mombasa to continue resting and waiting upon God. With all my heart I could now sing; "It is well, it is well with my soul..." Can you imagine my joy when I returned home to wait the unfolding of the plan of God for my life.

CHAPTER THIRTEEN

PACWA

As I write this book, I am the Continental Coordinator of PACWA. This is my seventh year in this ministry. This chapter is dedicated to this part of my life story in the Lord's ministry because I believe this is what the Lord had in His mind when He spoke about a specific women ministry, during the Kanamai retreat, which He wanted me to head. I believe too, this is one of the reasons why He took me through all the fiery experiences in order to make me suited to such a ministry. I see now that it wouldn't have taken anything less than going through the fire.

The PACWA International Council Members had a two - day fruitful meeting at the Silver Springs Hotel, Nairobi, Kenya on 2nd - 3rd June 1989.

The council consisting of 15 women and one male ex-officio member represented the steering committees of the five regions of Africa.

This was the final Pre-conference council meeting

intended to tighten all the loose ends, and consolidate the major programme plans. It was also to give a united direction towards the Nairobi Assembly and beyond the PACWA Assembly.

The prompt arrival and enthusiastic atmosphere surrounding council members told more than words could, what PACWA had come to mean in their hearts. "We are all here", exclaimed one council member excitedly as the group climbed the stairs to the meeting chamber. It had now become apparent that PACWA was going to be. The current council chairman had often said so as she motivated the women committee members. The PACWA vision was getting clearer and dimness was disappearing. The vigour with which the council members were approaching business and the shouts of joy was telling enough.

The representatives read out reports of Pre-PACWA consultations, and all the highlights were encouraging. Most importantly, all that the Pre-PACWAs envisaged did actually take place. The reward was beyond our expectation. By April 1989, six pre-PACWA regional seminars in all the six regions had taken place as had been planned. This was clearly the Lord's doing, considering all the hassles and obstacles such as the initial opposition and inter-church conflicts which characterized the beginnings of the plan. But all were levelled out sooner or later. Victory had been won. God's Spirit had touched women and nations. There was evidently a new spiritual dimension building up among the women across the continent

Some of the results

A male observer attending the West Africa Anglophone meeting asked, when PACWA could invite men? This was a clear indication that the women had something worth hearing by men.

The wife of Dr. Banana, the former President of Zimbabwe, was in attendance at the Southern Region Pre-PACWA and prayed for the conference taking place in Harare. President Mugabe's sister, also the women political party leader was in attendance at this meeting. I saw God's unsearchable wisdom. How else would these political leaders of the nations have been able to hear the gospel of Jesus Christ?

Both ecumenical and evangelical women were identified in the Harare conference.

The Vice President of the Church of Christ in Zaire attended the Pre-PACWA in Kinshasa. As an expression of his impression of PACWA, he wrote a letter calling for as many as possible to attend PACWA in Nairobi. Even the secular environment was not left untouched. The Pre-PACWAs in Accra, Ghana and Harare, Zimbabwe received full media coverage. So the nations heard that Jesus came into the world, died and resurrected to save mankind, for this was the core message intertwined in all other issues PACWA was tackling

The impact of Pre- PACWA, Harare, went as far as the Zimbabwe ministry of social affairs, who took it up through the initiative of the Government officials who participated in the seminar to open an official PACWA file in that ministry. Today that file is still on record. Further, a group of women in Bulawayo, Zimbabwe and in Zaire, initiated regular meetings of fellowship, prayer and discussion of topics covered during Pre-PACWA. These had a very wonderful impact on women, in their spiritual growth and stability in the Lord.

The Nairobi executive committee members vigorously met, planned and regularly prayed and fasted for PACWA.

During the Nairobi International Council meeting nominations for post-PACWA were spelt out. My name was proposed. I had now been serving in two capacities, as Chairperson of the Executive Committee and of the International Council. I was privileged to have two assistants elected. Mrs. Olive Taylor-Pearce (Sierra-Leone), who was resident in Kenya as Vice Chairperson of the Executive Committee and Mrs. Eva Sanderson of Zambia, as Vice Chairperson of the International Council of PACWA.

The time has come

For several months, I chaired the Executive Committee meetings to steer the planning of the PACWA conference. An exciting group of 12 women and I, plus Dr. Adeyemo as ex-officio, laboured in prayer and in consultations, in discussions, fund raising, looking and booking for venues and accommodation and in all relevant communications. I was not only chairing the executive committee but I had to oversee strategic sub-committees in charge of different aspects of this venture.

Finally our labours and prayers were rewarded when on Monday, 6th August 1989, the week-long PACWA continental conference began. The Kenyatta International Conference Centre was a beehive of activity. The Head of State, His Excellency, Daniel Arap Moi, the President of the Republic of Kenya officially launched the conference at 10:30 a.m. The continental conference attracted over 2,000 delegates from 38 countries in Africa and six observer nations from outside Africa. A timely PACWA theme song - "Our time has Come" had been composed by a Nairobi based Gospel Music Group. It gave an excellent impetus and a beautiful climate to the whole conference scenario.

From 8:00 a.m., the scene of the event was one to behold. Women had already started to arrive. Their attires, another sight to behold, represented the different localities of National to conventional dress, from East to West, North to South. The government security system was fully in force, Church and Christian organisation leaders and various Christian groups were all lined up to support PACWA and to welcome the President and PACWA guests. For us in the Executive Committee, we saw God honour His name among Christian women who had given themselves to declare His name among the great and small, the rich and the poor, the elite and the ordinary, believer and non believer.

The event, once again, touched both the secular and religious, and the whole Nation of Kenya heard and saw the glorious work of God, for it was covered live by the national television and radio. As if that was not enough, for the whole of that week, we had to find a way of coping with the numerous press interviews. It was like the whole press fraternity, local, international, private and national newspapers and magazine editors and reporters descended on the conference venue, not to mention after the event; still others followed to get more stories.

His Excellency took the microphone after the usual formalities and to the surprise, as well as affirmation to others, he confessed publicly that he was a born again Christian. In his launching speech, he assured the women that his government was in support of women among other things.

I had the opportunity to give a speech and take the privilege for the glory of God and share what the Lord was doing, in the hearing of dignitaries and in the hearing of the nation of Kenya. Excerpts of the speech highlighting some of the issues raised are reproduced here:

"... This Assembly, PACWA has become a reality! We call it unique because it is the first of its kind in the last 100 years of Church history in Africa. What is PACWA and what do women mean when they boldly announce 'Our Time has Come?' Does that mean they are no longer going to cook? This and many others may be some of the questions going on in many minds. Let me start by explaining what PACWA is ... It is a movement that will start with an event-indeed this Assembly. The purpose of this movement is to bring together leading evangelical Christian women from the whole of the continent of Africa, so as to examine national, continental and worldwide issues that we encounter in our lives as women. Such issues, for instance, include AIDS, witchcraft, polygamy, the plight of the widow and her children, poverty and hunger, evangelism, sex abuse, social injustice and battered women, just to mention a few.

... The time has come, therefore, for committed Christian women in Africa to unite our efforts to reach the nations of Africa for the Lord Jesus Christ. PACWA has a vision - to reach Africa for Jesus. So it is not time to compete with men but for us to complement each other ... PACWA is calling both men and women in the church and society to recognize that the calling and mission of Christ is extended to the total family of God.

Therefore, the theme 'our time has come' should not threaten anybody. It firstly challenges women to rise up to the call of God in Luke 23:28, 'But Jesus turning to them said, "Daughters of Jerusalem, do not weep for me, but weep for yourselves and for your children."' Women cry for your children. Did you ever realise that each person here is a child of a mother? If all mothers cry for their children, God will hear and hold back His wrath from our generation. It is also a challenge to Christians to lessen the tension between the sexes, to loosen chains that have bound women in the area of ministry and simply to recognize their potential. Working together in harmony will bring glory to God. But it is also time, for men to realize that we are God's latest models of creation - the model with least problems. So we are asking men to give us a chance, an opportunity to use our God-given abilities.

After this, I had many people calling me to congratulate and thank me for all the effort I had put into it. To us, who had struggled prayerfully and worked day and night, we saw something beyond the outward show. We saw and knew that God was at work.

A few days later, I remembered to look at the newspaper photograph that was taken as I marched beside the President towards the meeting hall. I couldn't hold my tears. Out of the inner recesses of my being, I saw something else, I saw a picture of all the pain, struggle, rejection, fear and doubts. I called to mind all that I passed through on the road to this reality. I realised God wanted to make me a vessel of honour, to the glory of His name, by making me suited to steer an event like this. In this pensive mood, something seemed to roll like a film, where I saw all the tears I had cried being wiped away. I saw the prophecies being fulfilled. And, I think I heard a voice saying that if I remain faithful, the Lord was going to fulfill His word to me. Looking back, this was just the beginning.

The Lord reminded me then, of all those times I wanted to exonerate myself. He made me to understand that if I had gone to court, as I had contemplated at one time when I was going through a crisis and misunderstanding, to prove my innocence before those who opposed my ministry, it would only have been known by a few people. He said that, He allowed me this privilege in order to exonerate me Himself, but He also said it was not for anything I had done, so I should never be proud.

I was so happy when a few years after that event, I was able to read in a book form all the papers that were presented in that conference, as well as the resolutions and covenant. The book entitled "Our Time has Come", which covers in detail this event, was published by the Paternoster Press in the UK.

One other significant thing that happened at the end of the conference week was the AEA Council meeting decision. At its conclusion the meeting recommended that AEA hire a full time Coordinator for the Women's Desk who would implement the PACWA resolutions.

All along, for the leadership of AEA and the PACWA Executive Committee, it was very clear that PACWA should not be just another conference, that would within a short time file away its papers and resolutions. The council was to give recommendation for the Women's Desk. There was an indication from the council members during this strategic meeting that, many had prayed individually and felt I should be appointed to take the position, and that they were going to "recommend" to AEA that I should be appointed!

That time, none of them had any idea that Dr. Adeyemo and I were praying for a suitable person and as yet, I still felt unsuitable myself. I loved the ministry, but continually felt unable to meet the demands of such a great responsibility. Now what could I say? Here I was again, terrified at the very thought. Even though I knew the Lord was preparing me for a ministry, I convinced myself it would be the Ladies Homecare Fellowship. To my delight, the council meeting ended without a final decision because, after all, they were only to recommend to the General Secretary of AEA, so I had more time to pray and think.

The recommendation was made. The General Secretary had been praying and according to the answer he got, I was the person. All my excuses and put offs were over-ruled and challenged through God's Word. The final nail as it were, was hit on the head through the word of Philippians 4:13. "I can do everything through Him who gives me strength".

On 2nd October 1989, I found myself at AEA offices to take up the position of PACWA Coordinator. A question, however, lingered on my mind - having now interacted with the AEA inner circles, I had now understood its financial status, was I ready to go into this ministry by faith? Didn't I wonder for a while, about my having to fore-go some of the conveniences, benefits and prospects that I had in my old job? I knew exactly what this implied- to resign from my executive position, from a highly paying job and lose all the prospects of financial security. Of course these thoughts were human. It would have been different had the Lord not dealt with me through His own school of preparation. But this had been settled between me and the Lord, the future didn't bother me any more. I knew He would take care of me. At last, by His grace, in October 1989, I was settled to handle the PACWA Desk.

The first few months in AEA set up were quite difficult. The adjustment was slow. For me it was not the big things that bothered me but the small ones such as not having a cup of tea at regular times and timely as I used to have, not having a messenger and driver at call at my service and convenience. I even had two secretaries. In my former office, I was so used to these privileges that it was almost a natural expectation. I found myself in this new situation, unable to believe life in the work place would be normal without those privileges. But I had to submit to God's new school again, to learn to lead a "missionary" life. I soon learned the lesson by His grace and I accepted this "calling" I did not, therefore, expect much in terms of salary. I had to be content in whatever situation, including a small office with an old conference table to be my desk.

Seven years later, I look back with a grateful heart to the Lord for His enabling power. He has done so much. The ministry has now reached 40 countries in Africa and has been officially launched in 28 of those countries including U.S.A. It is still growing in strength. Not to mention the spiritual and social impact it has had on the diverse categories of women. There are now women who have received skills training in various aspects who can earn an income. Other self help projects have been set up to help different communities of women to alleviate poverty. Best of all are the reports of the souls, which have found the Lord Jesus as their Saviour, either directly or indirectly through the PACWA programmes. I am grateful to the Lord and the AEA leadership for this privilege and opportunity to serve the women in PACWA.

When the Lord opens the door, He really opens it wide. I thought PACWA was the greatest challenge and opening that He would give me. I did not know He had other plans within this context.

CHAPTER FOURTEEN

THE CENTURY'S NEW CHALLENGE

One day in 1990, I had worked very hard and was looking forward to a restful evening. Coordinating PACWA work was proving to be more demanding than I expected. I was still adjusting to the world of full-time ministry.

Arriving home in the evening after a hard day's work, I heard the telephone ring. I was rather in a low mood and I hesitated to respond to it for a while. I threw my shoes off and for one moment, felt like telling my house-help to tell the caller I was not in. However, my conscience could not allow me to do this. I had finished teaching on a series of family life. In one of my topics, I was teaching on the importance of telling the truth. I had already shared that we are the role models for our children and that when we told lies they copied us. That reminder came in a flash of a second.

When I picked the phone, I realized there was an international connection and suddenly was glad I had not ignored it altogether. The voice on the other side came through and tried to establish whether that was indeed the Mbugua residence. I confirmed it was and the caller introduced himself. "I am Luis Bush, President of AD 2000. I was taken aback, for a moment I wondered whether I heard him right. It couldn't be! That year George Bush was the President of the United States of America. So the coincidence was quite strong. The man took a brief moment to explain what AD 2000 was. Finally he said they were looking for a lady to be chairperson of the Women's Track of the AD 2000 convention. He informed me that my name was given to them among six others and after praying they felt they would like to request me to serve in that capacity. He spoke for about 15 minutes explaining what was expected of me. Then he asked me, "Would you consider taking the position?"

I was glad he was far away, so could not see my face as I held that phone. As he talked I was going through some kind of shock. When I picked the phone I only heard the name President Bush of America. I was wondering what on earth I could have done that would cause a whole President of the United States of America to call me personally? So while Luis was speaking and taking so much time to explain his agenda I was soul searching. What could I have done, when, and where? I was completely lost until he asked the question, "Would you consider?"

Because I did not even hear clearly what I was supposed to consider and my heart was beating so fast, I asked him to put the information in a letter and post it. He said it was urgent. So he would rather fax it. The following morning, I found a 10-page fax on my desk. The fax revealed who this Bush was. The fax message also contained details of the vision and purpose of AD 2000.

I came to understand that the AD 2000 is a grand global evangelization vision being undertaken through the steering efforts of Key International Christian Leaders, and being planned in response to the Great Commission.

As I read through the fax, I agreed whole heartedly with the vision, yet I could not commit myself to take on further responsibility. I was already working with PACWA and the responsibility and expectations were overwhelming. I needed to give my best to PACWA, with undivided attention. But while talking with Luis Bush, he mentioned that they had been praying, so I felt the least I could do before I give my response was to pray - and pray I did.

I called my prayer partners and really prayed over this matter. In my heart of hearts, I knew I could not take such a heavy responsibility. In my prayers I would present names of women that I knew were so able: like Dr. Inonge Lewanika or Eva Sanderson. I named many others, but got no peace. I even tried to remind the Lord how unable I was, but heaven was silent.

While I was struggling, AD 2000 was waiting for my response. I shared the request and struggle with Dr. Adeyemo who promised to seek God on the issue. Luis and Lorry Lutz (Lorry is the International Coordinator of the Women's Track) were still waiting for my response. After several weeks they felt they could not wait any longer, and therefore sent Lorry to my office to have a real heart to heart talk with me.

By the time Lorry arrived, I had prayed and prayed, yet I was still fearful. Lorry held talks with Dr. Adeyemo. In their meeting, in my absence, the struggle I had over combining AD 2000 and PACWA, however, was sorted out. The AD

2000 Women track in Africa would be the Prayer and Evangelistic outreach of PACWA. AD 2000 would also be autonomous and would incorporate Christian women outside the evangelical persuasion, but they would always have one of their committee members at the PACWA Executive of the different countries, where PACWA was already established.

In the end, I did not have to give my answer. Dr. Adeyemo gave it on my behalf. With the above understanding, he felt that PACWA and AD 2000 Women's track stood to gain from this alliance. He said he had prayed a lot over this and he felt I should go ahead and take the responsibility. He pledged his personal support and that of AEA. He has lived to his word and given support, prayer, advice and time off as necessary.

My next challenge was to meet the AD 2000 women committee. They are International Women of God with great talents and experience. The list includes among others: Evelyn Christensen the renowned writer of "What happens when women pray", Dr. Inonge Lewanika, a member of parliament in Zambia and a woman of great faith and experience, Mrs. Juliet Thomas (India), Mrs. Robyn Claydon (Australia), Blossom White (Caribbean), Merfa Carbrera (Argentina), Elizabeth Mittlestaedt (Germany), editor of Lydia Magazine, and others; all giants of faith and women of great reputation.

Again I began to fret the possibility of chairing a meeting with such "giants". The first meeting was called in San Jose in USA. I decided to attend but requested that I serve as a committee member but not as Chairman.

However, on arrival, my job was made easier by the love

expressed among the ladies. We had not met before but the Lord knit our hearts and spirits together. We shared our experiences, ministries, prayed together and then drew the ministry agenda for the women's track. Within the three days, we made lasting friendships. I will forever be grateful to the Lord for allowing me to meet these "giants" of faith. I have learnt a lot from them, and together we are mobilizing international networks of prayer by women.

CHAPTER FIFTEEN

PROPHECY BEING FULFILLED

I Thessalonians 5:20- says, "do not treat prophecy with contempt. Whereas I cannot say I treated the prophetic word on my life with contempt, it would be right to say I treated it with caution. For example, there were those who prophesied that I should leave my local church, and others who prophesied that I would leave my secular employment at certain dates. These prophecies did not come to pass.

On the other hand those prophesies that promised "high" things made me scared. My attitude was like "wait and see". Many of the prophecies indicated that the Lord was calling me into global ministries, and He would take me before Kings and Princesses. I did not understand what that meant, but I marvel as I saw His plan unfolding, still by His grace and not merit. He has given me the opportunity to minister a lot locally and in Homecare, which now has 14 branches all over Kenya. He has allowed me to speak in many International meetings, where He has also given me an appropriate word for the moment.

Some of those conferences like, Destiny `92 brought together by African Americans, looking for ways to network and fulfill the Great Commission. The Lord gave me a word for the Church during that conference. The launching of PACWA in Kenya and other African countries brought together many African Church and Government leaders. During the launching of PACWA Madagascar in 1996 over 700 got saved and 30 Bible study groups began, which are growing strong in the Lord.

Trully, according to prophecies uttered concerning me, the Lord has given me the opportunity to "stand before and minister to presidents and princesses". I have spoken at a Presidential Breakfast meeting in Uganda at the invitation of the late Hon. B.K Kirya, Minister in the office of the President. It was a privilege to meet His Excellency President Yoweri Museveni of Uganda and the first lady Mrs. Janet Museveni, who has become a personal friend.

While launching PACWA Malawi, a few PACWA committee members and I had the privilege of meeting His Excellency Kamuzu Banda, the former president of the country, had lunch with him and had the privilege of being state guests. We were able to share the words of Solomon and the Queen of Sheba in 1st Kings 10:6,7 and challenge him to "taste and see that the Lord is good."

I would mention many more, except for the purpose of this book, but the last two include Global Commission on World Evangelization (GCOWE '95). This was an AD 2000 leaders' meeting held in Seoul Korea in May 1995. As the chairperson of Women Track, I was requested to represent the agenda for the Women's Track on "Dreams Women have for AD 2000.

As usual I was initially very scared as the time approached for me to speak in this grand conference. This fear I have come to realize, exposes how frail and helpless I am without God's help, and it makes me to totally rely on Him alone and not on my own understanding. "For without me you can do nothing" says the Lord.

The message was taken from the book of Mark 11:1-10, and was entitled "LOOSE THEM". The message was long but a few excerpts, with some slight editorial adjustments are reproduced here because I believe it has an impact and lessons for the church leadership today.

The introduction of this message is a quotation I came across in a magazine. I used it, not only as an anecdote, but a relevant pointer to the stereotype that can easily fit well with some existing and potential descriptions so easily relegated to women.

"I came across the following analysis of Jesus' disciples resume recently!"

"Thank you for submitting the C.V.s of the twelve men you have picked for managerial position in your new organisation. All of them have now taken our battery of tests and we have not only run the results through our computer, but also arranged personal interviews for each of them with our psychologist and vocational aptitude consultant.

The profiles of all tests are included, and you will want to study each of them carefully.

Most of your nominees are lacking in background, education and vocational aptitude for the type of enterprise you are undertaking. They do not have the team concept.

We would recommend that you continue your search for persons of experience in managerial ability and proven capability.

Simon Peter is emotionally unstable and given to fits of temper. Andrew has absolutely no qualities of leadership. The two brothers James and John, the sons of Zebedee, place personal interest above company loyalty. Thomas demonstrates a questioning attitude that would tend to undermine morale. We feel that it is our duty to tell you that Matthew has been blacklisted by the Greater Jerusalem Better Business Bureau; James, the son of Alphaeus, and Thadeaus definitely have radical leanings, and they both registered a high score on the maniac-depressive scale.

One of the candidates, however, shows great potential. He is a man of ability and resourcefulness, meets people well, has a keen business mind, and has contacts in high places. He is highly motivated, ambitious and responsible. We recommend Judas Iscariot, as your controller and right-hand man. All of the other profiles are self-explanatory.

We wish you every success in your new venture.

Sincerely Yours - Jordan Management!"

The main message for the women agenda was focused on the Triumphal Entry to Jerusalem; where Jesus is dramatically portrayed as King, riding on a colt in fulfillment of prophesy. I drew these lessons from reading this passage:

This colt, that Jesus rode, was still tied, yet it was ready for service. Immediately it was released, it did the very important task of carrying the Master.

Every colt that qualifies to carry a man should be in the field and not tied.

This colt was not productive because it was tied - not its fault, but none-the-less unproductive.

Tied very close to the gate - almost there - yet not there at all.

Jesus could have used a horse (more powerful and faster) but He chose to use a colt. If He chooses to use women, nobody should continue to tie them. (He needs every available resource to be released).

Jesus warned that if you untie the colt, the action would be challenged. Challenges should not stop us.

The above story can represent the situation of many people all over the world. In particular women and children the two most marginalized people groups in the world. Sadly, this is not only in the secular society but in the spiritual one too. Because they are tied:

a) They become the majority of the unreached i.e. Muslim World, Women Movement. Their accessibility is so restricted. In some places, women have no religion and they are forced to follow that of their husband.

b) They cannot reach the unreached. They are tied by:

  - Traditions and culture

  - Church and religious traditions

  - Fear

  - Family

  - Economy

Part of the summarised dreams would imply that once women are released, there would be increased results of the Lord's work, such as short-term missionary projects. Women would be willing and encouraged to move, once they are untied. They would get together to strategize and seek unique methods of evangelism. In the past, the serious mistake of leaving out women in the ministry was made especially because Ministry has been narrowed to pulpit ministry. This mistake should never be repeated.

In conclusion, the emphasis is; this colt was ordinary but was made special by carrying Jesus. It remained special as it continued carrying Jesus. The same is with all of us. We become special when we are being used by the Master.

CONCLUSION

How do you conclude a story of life that is still continuing? The ministry continues. Jennifer gave her testimony during the LHSF dinner, at the 10th anniversary of the ministry.

There is also the testimony of Wanjiru, a single mother and Mama Wambui, which are very touching, and of course numerous other testimonies abound. But to mention just briefly, Wanjiru is dead. Before she died she asked if we would like to keep baby Paul. Then she got ill and died before any plans were made. However, we in LHSF felt that Paul was our baby, and we have been able to identify where he is. LHSF has given support to him and now placed him in a home, awaiting adoption.

My own family now is a different story, the children are grown and I am the proud grand mother of two little girls named after me and one grandson. My sons took after their father in their careers. They are Certified Public Accountants. The Lord blessed them with good jobs - Praise the Lord. The first two are the fathers of both Ciirus. As for my daughters, the first is pursuing her phD in sociology at the Indiana University - U.S.A. The other is a designer. They have continued with the Lord even though some of them still go through the occasional Christian derailments.

Earlier in the book, you remember when I got saved, I was supposed to keep it to myself. As you have come along with me you realize I did not keep quiet, (not submissive you think!) but I leave you to judge. However, I want to say that I am ever so grateful to God for my beloved husband. He has been the best gift the Lord ever gave me on earth. He is my greatest supporter in the Ministry. He has continued to provide financially so that I am able to fuel the car, go to any part of the country for Ministry. At times he has accompanied me to different places while in Ministry.

People ask me, how do you travel so often and leave him? One day I asked him how it affected him and he said that he was the first one to witness the call of God in my life and he will do anything to support it. He has even promised to finance me should I ever opt to go to the University, though he thinks I am managing well without a University degree.

On my part I find it very difficult to leave him alone when I travel, especially overseas. Many times when he has taken me to the airport he has to wipe away my tears. I do not enjoy travelling and I miss him very much. I also miss my comfortable bed and usual food; but I realize I cannot give God that which costs me nothing. I am particularly lonely while on overseas travel and have to wait for hours for connections. Let me add that my greatest joy as I travel is when I share about the saving power of Jesus Christ. This is how I know I am in God's will and that His word prophesied earlier and decreed before I was born is being accomplished.

As I write this book my health is a matter of concern and prayer. Just when we were at the peak of organizing for the PACWA, I was diagnosed with a health problem for which I have to constantly be on medication. I am still on treatment in spite of much prayer.

The other day I went to Nairobi Hospital and as I was coming out and feeling sorry for myself and depressed with the results of my medical check-up a lady called my name. She came hastily, hugged me almost throwing me to the ground and said; "Praise the lord. Judy, look at the baby". I looked and there was nothing unusual. Then she said excitedly, "This is not even the first, this is the second," she continued; "Do you remember praying for me because I was barren? The Lord has opened my womb and now I have two children." That made my day. Though I was wondering why God has not heard my prayer and healed me, the testimony of this lady and the coincidence of meeting her right outside the hospital was a clear reminder that God hears and answers prayer.

In the recent past the Lord gave a vision to two of us in the LHSF concerning a Prayer Tower that would be built and used for intercession. We didn't know where it would be built or where the piece of land would be or even how to get the money for such an undertaking. As of now the vision of the Prayer Tower has partially been fulfilled and now we have a prayer room with a telephone and an office secretary. We have opened it for other groups who want to use it. The LHSF committee uses it every Thursday for prayer for Families, the Nation, the World evangelization and LHSF ministry.

Several people call me to say I have been a blessing or an inspiration to them and for this I praise the Lord.

As I have said in my introduction, writing or having your story written leaves you very vulnerable. But yet, so many people who have heard my testimony have asked me to write a book and share some of the lessons learned. I am still learning. So this is only to give a summary of some of the lessons. They all cannot be put in one book, but I have a few to share:

Lesson one:

God is a God of second chance. He so loves, that He gives each of us many chances. He gave Adam and Eve a chance when they sinned. Instead of destroying them, He sent them out of the Garden of Eden, giving them another chance to relate with Him. Even in their new situation, He made them clothes out of an animal skin. He loved them and wanted them to become what he wanted them to be right from the beginning.

For me, God gave me another chance and taught me that, problems can turn out to be opportunities.

Lesson two:

Since I was an "A" student and had parents who could afford my education, if I never had such problems as I had, I would never have understood what it takes for God to fulfill His purpose in ones life. I would not know God's power and intervention in my life. Now I do. When a woman comes home and tells me how hungry she is or what her family is going through, I understand. I already mentioned a lady who came to my home and told me that they had no food for several days, and that they would drink only water and sleep. She said that the previous night the child had vomited after drinking water and that was why she had come to my house so early to ask for food. If I had not known what it is to lack, as I very well know some of my personal inclinations,

I would have considered her a great nuisance. However, on this occasion, I gave her food and later led her to the Lord Jesus for salvation. She has grown strong in the Lord and some of her children have come to know the Lord too.

Lesson three:

Problems are part of life until we go to glory. Someone said to me the other day, "Are you not lucky your children are big and now you have no problems?" I said, "Yes they no longer give me baby problems, but they have adult problems." Some people too have come to me wanting to get into ministry because they admire what they see in some of us in the ministry. Those that I have been able to share with have also known about the joys as well as the problems. They know one has to count the cost before jumping onto the bandwagon.

Lesson four:

Nobody should give up or quit. Paul told Timothy to continue in spite of problems- 2nd Timothy 3:14. That is my message to all those who read this book, "Never give up. Continue. We will not be judged by what we began, but by how faithfully we persisted to the end."

Lesson five:

The challenges ahead as I see myself now in global ministries are many, but I know the Lord is with me. Therefore "I can do all things through Christ who strengthens me, Philippians 4:13." "Not by might, nor by power but by the Spirit, says the Lord."